*Routledge Revivals*

I0127897

# Juvenile Delinquency

Originally published in 1922, *Juvenile Delinquency* was written while the author was Director of the Ohio Bureau of Juvenile Research. He believed that juvenile delinquency could be prevented and therefore a large part of adult criminality could be eradicated. He states in the preface that the book does not tell you how this will be achieved: 'It contains no cut and dried solution. But ... it may help advertise the fact that there is a small body of people who think they see a ray of light in the darkness. ...'. Today it can be read in its historical context.

This book is a re-issue originally published in 1922. The language used and views portrayed are a reflection of its era and no offence is meant by the Publishers to any reader by this re-publication.

# Juvenile Delinquency

Henry Herbert Goddard

Routledge
Taylor & Francis Group

First published in 1922
by Kegan Paul, Trench, Trubner & Co. Ltd

This edition first published in 2025 by Routledge
4 Park Square, Milton Park, Abingdon, Oxon, OX14 4RN

and by Routledge
605 Third Avenue, New York, NY 10017

*Routledge is an imprint of the Taylor & Francis Group, an informa business*

**Publisher's Note**
The publisher has gone to great lengths to ensure the quality of this reprint but points
out that some imperfections in the original copies may be apparent.

**Disclaimer**
The publisher has made every effort to trace copyright holders and welcomes
correspondence from those they have been unable to contact.

A Library of Congress record exists under LCCN: 21020945

ISBN: 978-1-032-90448-1 (hbk)
ISBN: 978-1-003-55814-9 (ebk)
ISBN: 978-1-032-90455-9 (pbk)

Book DOI 10.4324/9781003558149

# JUVENILE DELINQUENCY

BY

## HENRY HERBERT GODDARD

DIRECTOR, OHIO BUREAU OF JUVENILE RESEARCH

LONDON

KEGAN PAUL, TRENCH, TRUBNER & CO., LTD.

BROADWAY HOUSE  68-74 CARTER LANE, E.C. 4.

## PREFACE

Man is a bundle of antinomies! On the one hand he is selfish, egotistical and ambitious: on the other hand he is careless and thoughtless of self, devoid of foresight and impractical. He spends his time accumulating materials with which to be happy in his old age; and is so careless of his health that he does not live to enjoy his acquisitions.

He is patriotic, social and planful for the future: but he utterly ignores much upon which the future welfare of his country and his descendants depends.

He sacrifices everything in a great war to make the world safe for democracy and neglects the internal conditions which if uncorrected will eventually make democracy impossible.

He slaves that his children may have education and wealth but he takes no precautions to ensure that the world in which his children will live shall be such that they can enjoy their education and their wealth.

He wants his children to be honest and law-abiding but he is content to send them forth into a world that is full of dishonesty and law breakers.

He keeps his children healthy; and then sends them forth to die in a world full of contagion.

He thinks he will keep aloof from the diseased and the dishonest; and then he spends his days among them buying and selling.

There are two million people in the United States who because of their weak minds or their diseased minds are making our country a dangerous place to live in.

The two million is increasing both by heredity and by training. We are breeding defectives. We are making criminals.

Our courts are picking up many thousands of delinquent boys and girls every year. A very small percentage of them ever are restored so as to contribute their share to the general welfare. The most of them are always a burden and many of them become our most dangerous criminals.

Why is this so?

Because we have made no effort to understand these children.

Pessimism? No, the foundation of optimism.

All this can be changed. Juvenile delinquency can be prevented. A large part of adult criminality can be eradicated.

This book does NOT tell how. It contains no cut and dried solution.

But that it may help advertise the fact that there is a small body of people who think they see a ray of light in the darkness: that it may, through the experiences described, the facts recorded, the points of view presented or the theories hinted at, enable some to see farther and perhaps truer, to work harder and with more courage is the hope of the author.

# CONTENTS

# Juvenile Delinquency

## CHAPTER I

### THE PROBLEM OF DELINQUENCY

A bit of wisdom usually attributed to Solomon
is expressed in the phrase: "Spare the rod and
spoil the child," or in the language of the King
James version: "He that spareth his rod
hateth his son; but he that loveth him chas-
teneth him betimes." A maxim probably expressing the most common attitude of adults
toward children and their misdemeanors. If a
child offends he must be punished, and the
older the child the severer the punishment, because of his greater responsibility. Studies of
the history of punishment show that the idea
of inquiring into the responsibility of the offender is an extremely modern notion. Though
we have outgrown the idea that insane adults
are possessed of devils, we in practice still
hold children who do wrong are "possessed"
and the demon can only be exorcised by dras-

tic means. In reality they are often as truly insane as are the adults and like them should receive treatment rather than punishment.

Originally everybody was held responsible or rather everybody was punished, for the question of responsibility was never raised. Gradually this has been changing in recent years. The insane are no longer held responsible, although just how much insanity there must be to excuse a person is often discussed and is often a difficult problem to solve. Later came the thought that children were not quite so responsible as adults and often some little leniency was shown them.

In this connection the famous case of Jesse Pomeroy of Massachusetts is interesting. Although convicted of the most atrocious murder of little children, and sentenced to be hanged, the New England conscience could not quite bring itself to the point of carrying out the decree. In those days so little was understood of the psychology of childhood that no acceptable excuse could be found for the boy's conduct but his sentence was finally commuted to "life imprisonment with solitary confinement." And for forty years Jesse Pomeroy has lived in the Charlestown jail carrying out this sentence. Not until four or five years ago was the rigidity of the punishment somewhat relaxed and he was allowed some of the privileges that are granted other prisoners.

But since the day of Jesse Pomeroy's conviction, approximately forty-five years ago, great progress has been made. Today we are beginning to ask: "Why?" Whenever a child or a juvenile commits an offense, we ask, "Why did he do it?" And we are beginning to accept the answer that he did not know any better or he could not help it. Moreover the day is not far distant when we shall ask this question not only of juveniles but of all offenders. In other words it will become the fundamental principle of all treatment of offenders, that there is a reason for their conduct. Not only that, but we are going farther yet. We are fast approaching the day when we shall realize that disease and defect, mental and physical, are conditions favorable to the commission of offenses against the public. We shall accordingly ascertain the mental and physical conditions of all people and recognize the fact that the persons suffering from abnormal conditions of body or mind are particularly liable to commit crime. The logical consequence will be that we shall take the necessary steps either to cure such sufferers or to place them where they will have no opportunity to commit offenses. Several facts recently brought to the attention of the thinking public are leading directly to this better order of things:

1. The growing conviction that children are the nation's greatest asset; that while children differ among themselves both by nature and nurture there are comparatively few who can not be made into more or less useful members of society if rightly understood and rightly managed.

2. We are beginning to realize that most of our thieves, prostitutes, swindlers, shiftlings, vagrants and other more or less vicious characters are not "necessary evils" that must be tolerated.

3. We are beginning to apply common sense and logic to the understanding of that much abused concept of "personal liberty." We are beginning to realize that William H. Anderson is right when he says:

"Personal liberty ends where public injury begins. There is a higher personal liberty, and that is civil liberty. A man has no personal liberty to sell rotten meat. He has no personal liberty to run his automobile on the left side of Fifth Avenue. He has no personal liberty to shoot off a revolver in a New York Square. There is no such thing as personal liberty unless the man is the sole inhabitant of a wilderness. Every man gives up what he calls his personal liberty in return for the benefits he derives from society."

May we not add to that that a man has no liberty to bring into the world children who are surely going to be diseased or idiots; that a man has no personal liberty to allow his children to run loose and acquire habits and practices that are a social menace   Anderson is right, "Liberty ends where public injury begins."

4.   We are learning that large numbers of people are not responsible for their acts because of lack of sufficient intelligence; and that the proportion of the population possessed of relatively low-grade or abnormal intelligence, is so great as to make necessary a complete revision of our ideas of responsibility.

Adequate appreciation of these facts leads to the formulation of the problem of delinquency somewhat as follows:

The development of the child into a useful member of society is an evolutionary process, dependent upon the interaction of two forces; the one ueting from within and the other from without.   The former being the inherited nature of the child; the latter his acquisition from his environment.   The former is again sub-divided into two groups:

A.   Those characteristics and tendencies belonging to him because he is a human being and in which we are all alike.

B.   Those special tendencies which are the peculiar characteristics of a particular stock or family.

Into what kind of a member of society a child will evolve depends upon the kind of inheritance he has and the environment in which he is placed.

Intelligence is an inherited possession common to all human beings. But *the amount* of intelligence belongs to the second sub-division, that is to say, it is the peculiarity of the stock or family. We may regard idiots as intellectual monstrosities and as such bar them from our discussion. Omitting these, all human beings have intelligence. A child may be born of such stock that he inherits only imbecile intelligence whereas another may be born of stock whereby he inherits intelligence so high that it is commonly spoken of as genius. Each of these types together with all the intermediate grades are more or less dependent upon the environment in which they are found. But they are by no means equally dependent. The intelligence itself may to a greater or less degree control the environment. Man is a motile and not a sessile organism, consequently the intelligent person may, and usually does, change a poor environment for a better one. Hence it often comes about that a child with good intelligence makes more out of a poor environment than a child of low intelligence can out of the best environment.

It happens that many of the characteristics and tendencies both those that are universal or which we have designated as human and those that are special or family traits are more or less anti-social, at least are antagonistic to the welfare of society as at present constituted. For example: sex interest and activity is a common trait possessed by all human beings. But as society is now constituted the unlimited gratification of this instinct leads to anti-social conduct,—to conduct that is detrimental to the welfare of the group.

Again the tendency to accumulate material possessions is a human characteristic possessed by all. But society is based upon what we call property-rights; hence the human tendency to get possession of every thing that one wants runs counter to the property-rights of the rest of the group. Likewise there is a common human tendency or instinct, as the psychologist calls it, to mislead or deceive others as to one's purpose and intention, for the sake of the individual's own comfort and happiness. This again leads to conduct that is incompatible with the social organization. If we are to live together each depending upon the other we must be truthful and not deceiving.

In a similar manner one might go through long lists of the tendencies and characteristics that are common to human beings. There is perhaps another list that would come under the head of "family traits." But of these little is known. It seems probable that some instincts are possessed in varying degrees by different family strains.

From this it follows that the evolutionary process of making a useful member of society out of the human child involves a constant modification and control of these inherited impulses. How is this brought about? By the environment and the inherited intelligence. The child who has inherited good intelligence and a good home, will be thoroughly taught what society requires of him and by means of his intelligence is able to understand the teaching and to control his conduct. The child of poor intelligence, on the other hand, is unable to understand the teachings, and consequently, does not make the effort to control himself. On the other hand the child of good intelligence but brought up in a bad environment, a bad home, where he is not taught what society requires of him, discovers no reason for modifying his natural tendencies. He, therefore, grows up an anti-social being. The child brought up in a home where he is taught no control over the sexual impulses becomes a libertine. The child brought up in a home where all are thieves grows, in accordance with his natural impulses, into a thief. Similarly with the other traits. This is inevitable and is inherent in the nature of man.

At this point comes in the question of personal liberty as contrasted with civic liberty,—Has society any right to say what shall be the environment of its youthful members who are evolving into future citizens?

Must we sit inactive and see the child develop into a thief for the lack of the environment necessary to modify his tendencies and make a useful citizen?

Must we be content to be constantly annoyed, disturbed and caused to suffer loss through the activity of a group of beings who have not intelligence enough to modify their natural instincts so as to be useful citizens?

Or shall we say that the group is more important than the individual, and if his natural environment is not doing for a child what it should, we will take him out of that environment and place him in a better one? Or if he has not the necessary intelligence to enable him to modify his natural tendencies, since we cannot give him intelligence nor develop it, we will place him in an environment where he at least can do no harm. This is the view that the more thoughtful people are beginning to adopt. It is only necessary to free ourselves a little more fully from the idea that all these anti-social people are "necessary evils," for society to take the whole problem definitely in hand and quickly solve it. It is true that in actual practice so far we have not got beyond the point of mere recognition of some of these facts in connection with our dealing with offenders. We are beginning to ask in the case of many juvenile offenders: "What is his heredity?" "What is his environment?" "How responsible is he for his act?" "What shall we do, not to punish him but to change his habits and protect society?"

This much at least is a beginning, and progress is often rapid when once we have conceived the plan. We must look forward to the day in a not too distant future when we shall not wait until children have committed misdemeanors but we shall be on the watch at least for all suspicious cases and make wise and careful provision for all those who upon examination prove to have the inheritance or the environment that is almost certain to lead to anti-social conduct. Those conditions that can be cured, those traits that can be modified must be treated for that purpose. Those cases that lack sufficient intelligence to profit by training or treatment must be placed in an environment where they can be harmless to society, harmless and happy in their own lives.

Looked at broadly we see that human society divides into two groups:

1.  Those who can take care of themselves and contribute something to the general welfare, and

2.  Those who must be cared for.

All indications are that the size of the latter group is rather appalling.  Social investigations in many places have furnished figures that are decidedly disturbing.

To cap the climax we have the results of mental tests in the army.  These show that 10% of the drafted army of 1,700,000 men had the intelligence of a ten year child or less, and were found too incompetent to be worth sending over seas.  Another group, 15% had about the intelligence of an eleven year old child.  Out of this 25% of the population we may very properly expect to find a very large number who must be cared for by the competent group.

How is this to be done?  The answer is not easy.  First of all, it cannot be done at once.  A plan must be evolved and then the machinery for carrying out the plan must be gradually developed.  The first step is for a group of socially minded citizens to get conscious of the problem.

After this the most obvious point of attack is through the courts upon those who have committed misdemeanors.  We already have the sentiment well developed, that misdemeanants are subject to treatment by society. They may be punished or cared for. They have by their offense lost their right to complete freedom of activity. We have only to rationalize our ideas of treatment to be able to make a good beginning.

The next step will be to realize that if treatment is justifiable, prevention is more justifiable. We shall then evolve methods of detecting potential misdemeanants and take proper steps to prevent the offenses.

We will now turn to see what is actually being done by one State in its efforts to solve this problem.

# CHAPTER II

The State of Ohio has two institutions which under the old terminology were called reform schools. They are the Girls' Industrial Home, at Delaware, Ohio, and the Boys' Industrial School at Lancaster. To these institutions the courts send their troublesome cases. The girls' home receives about five hundred cases a year and the boys' approximately twelve hundred. In August and September, 1912, a survey was made of the mentality of one hundred consecutive admissions at each of these schools, with the following results: Of the one hundred girls examined 59 were considered feeble-minded, 14 were called borderline, 13 were mentally retarded, 14 were considered of normal mentality. In the boys' school 46 were feeble-minded, 26 borderline, 11 retarded and 17 were thought to be normal.

Of this situation Dr. E. J. Emerick, Superintendent of the Institution at Columbus writes as follows:

"The results indicate that over 50% of the boys and girls committed to our industrial schools are in reality mentally deficient. These institutions have attempted to discipline and train the delinquents committed to them, and return them to society.

"Now in the case of normal children who get into trouble through bad surroundings, this is sound doctrine; and the Industrial Schools have done valiant service in setting these normal individuals on their feet.

"On the other hand, defective children cannot be reclaimed in this way. Institutional training and discipline may serve to cover their defects, but can never bring such children up to normal. To give defective delinquents training and polish, and then to turn them loose upon the community, is a moral as well as an economic blunder, the gravity of which should give every thoughtful person pause. Yet our Industrial Schools have had no alternative; children are continually coming into these schools; the Institution for Feeble-Minded is full to overflowing; the only course open is to send these defective delinquents out—on parole, it is true; yet the great number of these defectives who return time after time to these institutions, and later to the reformatories or penitentiary, proves that our system does not meet the situation with regard to this unfortunate class." (*Problem of the Feeble-Minded*, page 6.)

To meet the situation thus disclosed as well as to help solve other problems connected with juvenile delinquency and abnormality the Bureau of Juvenile Research was established July 1, 1914, under the Board of Administration. Significant sections of the law establishing this Bureau are as follows:

Sec. 1841-1. *All minors* who in the judgment of the juvenile court, *require State institutional care and guardianship* shall be wards of the State, and shall be committed to the care and custody of "The Ohio Board of Administration," which board thereupon becomes vested with the sole and exclusive guardianship of such minors.

Sec. 1841-2. "The Ohio Board of Administration" shall provide and maintain a "Bureau of Juvenile Research," and shall employ competent persons to have charge of such bureau and to *conduct investigations*.

Sec. 1841-3. "The Ohio Board of Administration" may assign the children committed to its guardianship to the "Bureau of Juvenile Research" for the purpose of *mental, physical* and *other examination, inquiry* or *treatment* for *such period of time* as *such board may deem necessary*. Such Board may cause any minor in its custody to be removed thereto for observation and a complete report of every such observation shall be made in writing and shall include a record of observation, treatment, medical history, and a recommendation for future treatment, custody and maintenance. "The Ohio Board of Administration" or its duly authorized representatives shall then assign the child to a suitable *state institution* or place it in a family under such rules and regulations as may be adopted.

Sec. 1841-4.  Any minor having been committed to any state institution *may be transferred* by such ''The Ohio Board of Administration'' to any other state institution, whenever it shall appear that such minor by reason of its delinquency, neglect, insanity, dependency, epilepsy, feeble-mindedness, or crippled condition or deformity, ought to be in another institution.  Such Board before making transfer shall make a minute of the order for such transfer and the reason therefor upon its records, and shall send a certified copy at least seven days prior to such transfer, to the person shown by its records to have had the care or custody of such minor immediately prior to its commitment; provided, that, except as otherwise provided by law, no person shall be transferred from a benevolent to a penal institution.

Sec. 1841-5.  ''The Ohio Board of Administration'' may receive any *minor for observation* from any *public institution* other than a state institution, or from *any private charitable institution or person having legal custody* thereof, upon such terms as such Board may deem proper.

I quote again from Dr. Emerick who was the first Director of the Bureau:

''The Bureau aims to make a thorough examination of the child—mental, physical, and bio-sociological—

with a view to determining for each individual what disposition of the case is best for the child and for society.

"By means of mental tests and careful observation study by trained psychologists, the Bureau aims to find the defectives and future psychopaths while they are yet young and is then in a position to devise ways and means to control their lives. Just what these means are to be, must differ with individual cases; but we believe that in the case of criminally inclined defectives, and defective girls of child-bearing age, the cheapest, safest, and best solution lies in permanent custodial care. We have the majority of the idiots and low-grade imbeciles already segregated; and to segregate these higher-grade defectives would not add any great burden to the State, as they can be made practically self-sustaining under guidance.

"The medical phase of the work offers a wide field for study. Physical defects will be studied and treated; the relationship between delinquency and syphilis, as well as other infections, will be carefully studied; and many special problems whose solution would be of great value to the medical profession, may well be worked out.

"The bio-sociological phase of the work is also important. Careful field studies of the family history, the home conditions and general surroundings, and the personal history of the individual, should be made, particularly in the cases of no clear intelligence defect, or of doubtful intelligence defect. Such investigation should be valuable in determining whether the child would be likely to make good in a home. A normal child ought not to be institutionalized; and a *normal child should make good under the right surroundings*. The field worker should also, in time, accomplish a pretty thorough survey of the bad stocks of the state, through a study of the family history of inmates of our state hospitals, feeble-minded institution, and correctional institution.

"But the Bureau can do little unless additional buildings are provided to take care of the defective delinquents who require permanent custodial care. It is of no use to decide, 'This child should have permanent care' unless there is some place to send him where he can be cared for permanently. To this end, therefore, we need additional buildings for the feeble-minded. It is folly to say we cannot afford them; as a matter of fact, *we cannot afford not to have them. It is estimated that the trials and commitments of Cincinnati's feeble-minded delinquents alone cost the city and state over $2,597,468 a year!* From this it is evident that *these defectives will be cared for, one way or another; and they are being cared for at large at far greater expense than they would occasion in a custodial institution, where they would be happy, harmless, and practically self-sustaining.*

"When we realize that feeble-mindedness is not curable by any known means; that it is a hereditary condition in the vast majority of cases; that two feeble-minded persons can have only feeble-minded children; that the families of the feeble-minded tend to be larger than the average family; and that *from the defective progeny of our present defectives will be recruited in large measure the paupers, prostitutes, and criminals of the next generation*—when we come to a full realization of these facts, we shall see that money spent in attacking this problem is a most wise investment; and that a niggardly disposition of the matter now will saddle upon the next generation a burden at whose weight we shall be justly reproached.''

Unfortunately the legislature which passed the law creating the Bureau neglected to appropriate any money for its material equipment. The Board of Administration was able to appropriate certain funds for salaries; and offices were provided first at the Institution for Feeble-Minded and later in the Board's own building.

Under the circumstances nothing could be done in getting at the real work intended for the Bureau. But under the leadership of Dr. Thomas H. Haines, Clinical Director of the Bureau, much excellent preliminary work was done in the way of making surveys, establishing standards and collecting data for future reference.

The Legislature of 1917 remedied the defect by appropriating $100,000.00 for buildings in which to carry out this important work. Those buildings are now completed. They comprise: a laboratory building 40 x 80 feet, two stories with basement; two cottages, one story with basement, calculated to accommodate from forty to sixty children each. One is for boys, the other for girls. The buildings were hardly begun before war prices began to prevail with the result that the plant could not be entirely completed and kept within the appropriation.

In anticipation of the enlarged facilities for work the Bureau began in September, 1918, to somewhat extend its activities: The present Director was appointed in May, 1918, and in September the staff comprised besides the Director, a psycho-clinician, a physician and an assistant psycho-clinician and a clerk.

Other workers and assistants were added until in 1920-21 there were ten scientific workers, six clerks and stenographers and nine caretakers in the cottage department.

July 1, 1921, Ohio adopted the centralized form of government and the Board of Administration was replaced by a Director of Public Welfare. In anticipation of this change a temporary Board of Administration laid extensive plans for the enlargement of the work of this Bureau.

Although the Legislature did not approve to the extent of voting the necessary funds the new Director of Public Welfare plans to materially extend the work.

The proposed budget for 1921-2 provided for a psychological group of eleven members, a medical group of six, a cottage group of twelve caretakers and an adequate clerical force.

It is the plan to provide such personnel and equipment as may be found necessary for making thorough mental, physical and social investigations. The scope of the work of the Bureau as originally planned is indicated by the following proposed staff:

Mental examiners and diagnosticians,

Psychiatrists to study mental diseases,

Physicians for physical examinations and treatment,

Bio-chemists for the study of physiological processes with perhaps emphasis on glands of internal secretion,

Neurologists, pathologists, histologists, dentists, surgeons, X-Ray specialists and such others as may be found necessary to attack the problems involved in juvenile delinquency and abnormality.

It will be seen that we conceive our problem to be nothing less than the putting of these children into the best possible condition to live lives of happiness and comfort for themselves and usefulness to society—in other words these children must be saved, not punished.

It was estimated that eventually we should have to handle 4,000 cases a year from the courts—cases of serious delinquency the causes of which must be discovered in order to prescribe treatment. It was also expected that we should keep these children under observation as long as necessary to diagnose the case. The time needed varies greatly. The simplest case is that of plain uncomplicated feeble-mindedness. Such a diagnosis is as a rule easily made and when made fully explains any delinquency of which the child has been guilty. Such cases need stay in our observation cottage only a few hours. Perhaps the most difficult case is that of the seemingly normal child in whom no disease, mental defect or obviously bad environment can be found These cases often require long observation and study. Nothing is more sure than that there is a *cause* for the delinquency. It is equally certain that it is worth while both from the standpoint of justice to the child and the welfare of society, to find the cause no matter how much time and effort it takes.

Between these two extremes there are many grades of difficulty of diagnosis. For example: The psychopathic cases may give some symp-

toms upon the first examination, but often it is
necessary to observe them for days, weeks or
even months before it is clear just what is the
condition and what is best to be done. Similarly when the delinquency is suspected of
being due to the environment, the effect of a
new environment must be tried. Perhaps plac-
ing in a new home is indicated. But if so we
must keep in our observation cottage until we
are reasonably sure that it is safe to place in a
private home.

After two years of extended work the
Bureau finds itself facing several difficult
problems. First is our inability to assign the
cases to suitable institutions when we have
made a diagnosis. The Institution for Feeble-
Minded is full, consequently when we find a
child is feeble-minded there is nothing to do
but return him to the court whence he came.
Thus instead of relieving the judge of his burden, it is only made more difficult for him since
no one wants a feeble-minded child.

The number of these feeble-minded children
is much larger than we thought. Several states
have made careful surveys of their defectives
and the number found is from one-half to two
per cent of the population. These estimates,
however, include the group of psychopathic
children (which we will discuss later). The

Governor of New York said recently that New York State had forty thousand feeble-minded who needed institution care. New York has twice the population of Ohio. On the same basis therefore Ohio would have twenty thousand. If we halve this number we are surely safe in estimating that Ohio has ten thousand feeble-minded persons needing institutional care. These could not all be located at once even if we had the facilities. But it is safe to say that Ohio should provide for approximately two thousand a year for the next five years.

It is possible that such a program would solve the problem for it is now believed that a large proportion of the high-grade defectives need only five to ten years of such training as an institution for the feeble-minded can give them, in order to render them safe to send back to their respective communities as fairly useful citizens. They will need, to be sure, constant oversight by some sort of probation system. But experience seems to show that with a little guardianship such trained persons get along fairly well. The explanation is that the years of training in the institution fasten upon them a set of good habits which keep them straight and from which because of their very feeble-mindedness they cannot break away. Their chief danger is from evil minded persons who may influence them to wrong doing. But this danger the probation officers or after-care committee can largely avert.

In this connection it may be suggested that the conception of the institutions for feeble-minded might well be changed. They should no longer be custodial homes for imbeciles. They should be simply the "State Schools." Like.all schools they should have their courses of training which when completed entitle the child to "graduation"—not in an academic sense it is true and not to higher schools or to "business" but to an humble place in the community able to earn their own living and to fill their small niche in the world. Those who cannot "graduate," automatically become custodial cases; while the few who graduate but cannot get along at large must go back to the simplified environment of the institution to become useful workers in helping care for the lower grade cases.

The thought of institutions for feeble-minded as places of simplified environment should be cultivated in the public mind. These feeble-minded of higher grade are merely persons who cannot adapt themselves to the complexities of modern life therefore the State provides a community where they can live under more simplified conditions, the complexities being cared for by the intelligent care-takers. Many a father and mother with a family of normal children, feel that the city is too dangerous for their children, and so they move to the simpler conditions of the rural community. Or if they cannot do that, the children must still be kept from the traffic of the street and are "committed" to the back yard where they have their plays and games and even their work, and where they are safe and happy. The institution is the big back yard for the great group of people who for lack of development are always children.

Carrying the figure a little farther, the back yard is within easy reach of the parents. Similarly each social community should have its place of simplified environment for its undeveloped citizens. Perhaps when the social consciousness is more highly developed this will be the case and every community will attend to its own social problems. But at present it is the custom to turn this problem over to the State. Nevertheless no effort should be spared to elicit the interest of each community in its own defective children and in their welfare and happiness in the State Institution. Only thus will the best results be obtained. To the extent that the community turns its defectives over to the State and *forgets them,* the final solution of the problem of feeble-mindedness is put off to the distant future and the relief we seek from this burden is not forthcoming.

# CHAPTER III

As a further result of our three years of work we have discovered an unexpected problem in the psychopathic child. A number of difficult problems grow out of this one.

Psychopathic children differ from the feeble-minded in that the former are diseased while the latter simply have not developed. Psychopathic means *mentally suffering*—having a diseased brain. Such *mental disease* in an adult is called insanity. In children the disease is usually in its very incipient stages. Except in rather rare instances these psychopathic children do not have hallucinations, insane delusions, manias and other recognized symptoms of insanity. Their diseased condition is only to be determined by the most delicate measurements of mental capacity, tests and observation of mental functioning. Formerly diphtheria was often not diagnosed until the membrane was formed in the throat and the case was hopeless, but now there are various "tests" physiological or microscopic in character and so delicate that the layman can hardly understand them even yet. In the same way science has developed "tests" that reveal the psychopathic condition at a very early stage. The value of this discovery is the same as in the illustration —the greater possibility of cure.

This group therefore is at once on a different footing from the feeble-minded. The latter require care and training; the former require treatment.

No greater contribution to the problem of delinquency has ever been made than the concept of the psychopathic child. To whom belongs the honor of discovering the psychopathic child we do not know. It is certain that the idea did not spring full-fledged from the brain of any one individual. Some one, possibly more observing than the rest, suggested the term and gradually students of childhood have added to the picture until today the picture of the psychopathic child, while probably far from complete, is sufficiently adequate to enable us not only to talk about it intelligently but to apply it in a practical way to the problem of delinquency.

The type has been more or less definitely recognized for considerable time and under the name of the unstable child, the constitutional psychopath and various other terms, has often been mentioned.  But until recently little information has been forthcoming relative either to his origin, his characteristics or his treatment; moreover he has often been confused with other types.

A generation ago all children were classified into good children and bad children; of the good children little was said, they took care of themselves and needed little attention from adults; but the bad child was the object of constant though usually misguided effort.  It should be mentioned in passing also that the very classification into good and bad was highly arbitrary; for many people that child was bad who did not behave in the way the particular observer thought he should.  Moreover if a child did wrong according to anybody's definition, he was never excused on the ground that he did not know any better or that he could not help it, except in the case of very young children and idiots.  And it is possibly safe to say that it is to the idiots that we owe much of our present knowledge of childhood delinquencies and defectiveness.

When in 1905 Binet gave us the first suggestion for tests of intelligence, and in 1911 his perfected scale, the concept of feeble-mindedness became greatly extended.  It was soon discovered that there were irresponsible people all along the line. In the first enthusiasm of this great discovery many illogical conclusions were drawn. For example it was found that there were no persons in institutions for the feeble-minded with mentality higher than twelve years. From this it was concluded, illogically as will be seen, that all persons of a mentality of twelve years or less must be feeble-minded. Again when the tests began to be applied to children in reform schools and adults in prisons, and a good many of them were found to have a mentality of twelve years or less it was promptly concluded that they were feeble-minded and for a time it was thought by some that in feeble-mindedness we had discovered the source and cause of most of our social evils. While there was vastly more truth than falsity to this it was, never-the-less, an exaggeration; but it tended to cure itself by leading to a more careful study of the anoma-lous cases. It was soon discovered that our social problems were not entirely solved. For there were many cases that could not by any possibility be classed as feeble-minded by any of our tests. These cases were often noticeably peculiar but in what their peculiarity consisted or what was the cause we did not yet venture to suggest.

When it came to youthful misdemeanants it was of course easy to pass them on as merely "bad children." But to those who had come to recognize that many misdemeanants were irresponsible because of feebleness of mind it had become a fixed belief that for all misdemeanors there is a reason. Now it happened that in 1910 Dr. Rosanoff published his study of association in insanity. This study proved conclusively that the record of free association was an extremely delicate measure of the functioning of the mind. The free associations of a patient to one hundred selected words became, as it were, an X-Ray picture of his mind. But like the Radiogram, the list of associations had to be interpreted and it has taken some time to arrive at an understanding of the meaning and significance of the various associations. But it was not long until a careful study of results of this method gave us the measure of the abnormal functioning of the mind. When this test was applied to those misdemeanants who were at first thought to be feeble-minded but who did not show this on the test for feeble-mindedness, it was found that they showed marked deviations from normal mental functioning. It was at the Ohio Bureau of Juvenile Research that Dr. Florence Mateer applied this method to the study of the delinquents that were sent in by the Juvenile Court. Other tests were added later; but out of this the picture of the psycho-

pathic child had begun gradually to develop in a
definite and consistent way. It was found that
we could clearly differentiate not only between
the normal child and the feeble-minded but between the normal and the psychopath, between
the psychopath and the feeble-minded and even
pick out those cases that, while fundamentally
feeble-minded also had abnormal functioning
of their weak minds; that is to say were
"psychopathic feeble-minded."   And in the
report of the Bureau for the two years ending
July the first, 1920, will be found a classification
employing the various combinations of normality, feeble-mindedness and psychopathy.

Having found then what we call the psychopathic child as a type shown by various psychological tests, our next question is, "what are
the social characteristics?"

These characteristics are found to be no less
marked and definite than the psychological
peculiarities.   The child is usually nervous,
though not always in the sense in which that
term is popularly applied.   He is often forget-
ful and more or less disobedient according to
the degree of the abnormal functioning.   In the
more serious cases he may display a high degree
of cunning or shrewdness: is a persistent
truant, many times a persistent thief or klepto-
maniac, a liar and, in the worst cases of older

children, many times a persistent sex pervert or extremist. This is particularly noticeable in the girls. For a fuller description of this phase of the subject we will let Dr.˙Mateer speak, to whom belongs the credit for working out this whole problem.

"The major symptoms are similar in most of the cases although they may show very different phases. These children are frequently solitary. They do not get along with other children of the same mental level. If they are feeble-minded psychopaths they do not get along with the other feeble-minded children who are not psychopaths. The same is true of a psychopath of normal intelligence level among other normal children. Psychopaths are apt to prefer the company of adults, or in deteriorative cases, of low grade imbeciles. Their games have a queer monotony which not infrequently makes even the family realize their peculiarity. They are especially apt to have strong likes and dislikes as regards food. Those of the lower grades are usually destructive with toys, clothing and sometimes with anything they grasp. They are apt to have violent tempers and have often been recognized as 'different from the time they were born.' They may be moody. Most of them tend to be more easily depressed than to be pleasurably excited although the 'exalted' case is sometimes met with. These children meet Stanley Hall's description of individuals living at the ambivalent extremes of the emotional plane without enough emotional resiliency to swing back into a normal mood. Psychopaths are not usually fond of other children or pets and they may be quite cruel. They are apt to have queer hobbies. They are apt to sleep poorly and often suffer from night terrors.

"They may get along fairly well in school until they reach the third or fourth grade or even until they reach high-school, although other cases of early psychopathy are often inferior from the very beginning of school days. Relatively the psychopath is most apt to be poor in geography and spelling. These children are usually difficult to handle in the regular grade. Every schoolroom has one or more of them. They are the children on whom the teacher cannot rely and concerning whose misbehavior she is always concerned for they are different and rules and punishments never seem to fit.

"Compared with other children of the same mental level, whether these are feeble-minded children or normals, the psychopathic child is unreliable. He is very apt to lie fluently. He is apt to be a runaway. It is far harder to predict what a psychopath will do when put into a definite situation than it is to foretell the behavior of even an unintelligent but normal-functioning child."[*]

The next question that arises is: what are the causes of this abnormal functioning of the brain? Here as always when it is a question of cause we must proceed slowly and in this case

[*] *Journal of Delinquency*, January, 1921, p. 291.

we have to admit that as yet very little is known.
Whether there are hereditary types of psychopathy is an open question.   Biologically of
course there could not be such a thing since we
are dealing with function and not with structure.
But since our conception of psychopathy may
not be absolutely accurate, it remains possible
that there are peculiar nervous constitutions
which at least behave like these psychopathic individuals.   We do know of at least one congeni
tal condition.   So many of these children whom
we have studied are victims of congenital
syphilis and these show such marked and typical
indications of psychopathy that while perhaps
it is too soon to make an actual statement yet
one may say that it seems almost conclusive that
the congenital syphilis has caused the condition.
There would seem to be no objection to such
findings if the facts bear it out, since it is well
known that the poison of syphilis is highly selec-
tive and in the case of neuro-syphilis the various
parts of the nervous system are attacked.   And
in accordance with the well known law we would
expect that the nerve cells of more recent origin
would be the ones to be first affected and these
undoubtedly would be the cells of the cortex and
specifically of the layers and areas of the cortex
that have to do with the so called higher mental
processes—the   process   through   which   we

acquire control over the more primitive instincts.

Other environmental causes may be various diseases incident to the child himself such as some of the fevers, infections or intoxications. A mild condition of psychopathy (whether properly to be grouped with the more serious forms or not is still in doubt) seems to be traceable to disturbance of the emotional system, which of course may act through the glands of internal secretion affecting the blood stream and thus the brain itself. Fright from abnormal experiences, worry and perhaps over-work are illustrations. At least we find some children whose minds according to the tests are not functioning normally and in whom the parents have noticed certain mental peculiarities and upon whom school life seems to be weighing heavily. In these cases the removal of the condition as for instance taking the child out of school for a period, results in an abatement of the symptoms. This is not infrequently the case with exceptionally bright children, whom of course everyone is anxious to push ahead with the result that oftentimes they are overburdened and their minds thus subjected to a strain which they cannot quite carry. Abnormal functioning results. Such psychopathy may not have any connection at all with delinquency especially if it is recognized and cared for in time. On the other hand it is entirely possible that some of the wayward boys and girls in our best families have been cases that have begun in the way just described, but the condition not being recognized has gone on from bad to worse until serious misdemeanors have resulted.

At this point it will be helpful to consider the question of just why abnormal mental functioning shows itself especially in misdemeanors. In brief it is because the actions which we call misdemeanors are those which result from more primitive impulses and are uncontrolled in these cases by the higher mental processes. We shall take this up more fully later on.

What we call a mind normal in its functioning, reacts in very definite ways to particular stimuli. Contrary probably to popular belief the range of action in a given situation is for the normal mind comparatively limited. We have been in the past misled in this particular as is shown by the off-hand remark when a child does something which thoroughly intelligent people recognize at once as abnormal, somebody is sure to exclaim, "O that is all right, I have seen many children do that." In other words because we have seen many children do a great many things we conclude that normality must be stretched so as to cover this wide range of response. As a matter of fact psychopathy in children is so prevalent that we may expect to see much abnormal behavior and must not therefore conclude that because it is common it is to be considered normal.

In other parts of the body aside from the brain we are quite familiar with the principle of specific reaction to a specific stimulus. A gentle blow on the patella tendon produces a kicking of the foot. The absence of such a kick or a highly exaggerated kick are both taken as symptoms of abnormal conditions. The drawing a pin along the sole of the foot makes the toes curve downward; if the response is an upward turn of the toes instead of downward it is recognized at once as a symptom of an abnormal condition of the reflexes known as Babinski's sign. Blood when it comes to the air, coagulates; if this does not take place it is abnormal. Of course these are enormously simple situations compared to what we term a situation in which a human being may be placed and where he has to act. Nevertheless the more complex situation is only a combination of units. It is normal for a young child to cry out with pain and for an older one to make more or less successful effort to control such an outcry. It is normal for any one old or young having suffered pain and discomfort as a consequence of some act to carefully avoid that act in the future. Consequently the per-

sistence by a child in a line of action after repeated punishment therefor, is indicative of abnormal functioning of the brain.  To put it
another way the given situation does not mean
to the abnormal child what it does to the normal
child because his brain cells do not convey the
impression in the right order or the right direction or with the right amount of energy.  The
discovery of a gold ring lying on the table means
to the normal child who has been taught, that
someone has forgotten a ring; that he must
either let it alone or seek to find the owner and
restore the property.  To the abnormal child
the same situation with the same training and
perhaps even more experience as to punishment, the sight of the ring means only: grab it
and run.  We are apt to say in such a case that
he had every reason to know that it was wrong,
that he would be caught and punished and that
in the end he would be sorry.  As a matter of
fact we are probably wrong in our reasoning.
All we can logically say is that a normal child
would have those thoughts and feelings.  In this
particular case the child has no reason to know
these things because the brain cells are not functioning properly and the situation does not
mean to him what we assume that it means.

It is self evident that the psychopath is an irresponsible, non-adjustable, uncontrollable mis-
fit in society.  And must we add to that, incur-

able? In some cases probably yes, but fortunately many of these psychopathic children are so slightly affected that it does not prove a serious handicap. Some of them clearly outgrow the condition; others remain possessed of the peculiar characteristics of the mild psychopath throughout their lives. They are the strange, peculiar, erratic people that everyone notices but is not quite willing to call insane. They are often troublesome but not usually seriously so. Then there is the third group that rapidly deteriorates into some definite form of insanity.

The question, what is to be done with these psychopathic children, is as difficult as it is important. There is no denying that we should have children's psychopathic hospitals where these cases could be thoroughly and effectively studied to the end that we may first of all know more about them, be able to classify them; and secondly, discover, if possible, some treatment that will result in at least ameliorating the conditions if not in producing a complete cure. Many of these children are now in institutions for feeble-minded having been sent there because of their low mentality. They were confused with the purely feeble-minded children. There is perhaps no serious objection to this

procedure since having deteriorated to a low
mental level there is practically no hope that
any kind of treatment will restore them to
normality any more than it can the true feeble-
minded.  They complicate somewhat the problem of management and training for the feeble-
minded but once the officers of our institutions
understand the classification and recognize the
difference between the defective psychopaths
and the true feeble-minded, methods and work
can be adjusted to fit each group with a minimum of loss of effort.

It is the psychopath who has not deteriorated
but has a normal level or even, as many of them
have, a superior level of intelligence that constitutes the great social problem.   Such a
psychopathic child has all the skill and ability
of the normal person but without any control or
any regard for the social conventions, consequently he yields to his deeper and more
primitive impulses: becomes a thief, a liar, a sex
pervert or other troublesome person.   In short
he is not fit to be loose in a community; and
society cannot tolerate him.   Consequently he is
arrested and brought into court, but not being
feeble-minded, nor insane as the law recognizes
insanity he is only *bad* and therefore subject for
punishment.   He is committed to prison in the

expectation that the punishment will reform
him. In a sense it does reform him, that is to
say, he feels the force of the punishment and
resolves he will hereafter live straight. Under
the close surveillance of prison authorities he
behaves himself and therefore is quickly a
candidate for parole, brought before the parole
board he makes a strong impression. He has
good or superior intelligence, can frequently
talk well, he has repented, he means exactly
what he says and consequently when he argues
his case and makes promises of good behavior
he is tremendously convincing and it is no won-
der that pardon boards and governors yield to
these appeals and the individual is pardoned.
The only flaw in the whole procedure is the fundamental fact that he has a mind that does not
function normally. Consequently although he
means all that he has said, all his promises, yet
when he gets out and gets into the new situation,
his mal-adjusted mind fails to react properly
and the first thing that is known he is again before the court. To the court and court officials
he is merely a second offender and he goes back
to jail with an increased sentence. And so it
goes on. Children have been brought to the
Bureau of Juvenile Research who have been in
the Boys' Industrial School at Lancaster four

and five times.   Clearly the right treatment has
not been found.

What is the right treatment?   There is no
satisfactory answer to the question.   If science
ever discovers any way to cure the condition
itself, that will of course solve the question.   But
in the meantime it would appear that the only
thing to be done is to deal with the condition as
best we may.   It would seem that the first important procedure is to acquaint the patient
himself with his condition, at least in all cases
where he is old enough to appreciate it and to
have a temporary desire to overcome it.   The
man who knows he has a weak heart is usually
more or less cautious as to how he takes violent
exercise.   The man who knows he has digestive
troubles, although his appeti   frequently leads
him astray never-the-less undoubtedly saves
himself from much illness by the control he
exercises in the matter.   So in these cases it is
feasible and seems indicated, in some cases at
least, to say to the patient: You have a brain
that does not function normally.   Situations
that lead other boys and girls to do the things
that make their associates respect and honor
them, are apt to lead you to do things that bring
you into disgrace, or before the law.   Now while
you cannot change your brain you can do much
to keep yourself from reacting in the way that

will bring trouble to you. In the first place you
can think about it and avoid getting into those
situations; secondly when you are in such a situation you can try to think how other people
would act and do your best to compel yourself to
act the same way.

Of course, each case has its peculiarities and
while one cannot prescribe the kind of suggestion that is best in each case, we have found that
these morale talks are of considerable value to
these young people. And after they have left
us we attempt to keep up the influence by weekly
or monthly letters repeating the same idea in
perhaps changed form but with the purpose to
constantly keep hold of these children, showing
our interest in them and reminding them of the
things that their diseased mind is so apt to
forget.

The study of this problem from this angle is
so new that there is very little inference to be
drawn from experience. We may very well expect however, that the law of habit applies in
these cases as in others and that many times a
change of environment, thus breaking up old
habits and associations, may have considerable
value and bring about desirable results.
Especially is this true if the new environment is
such as to firmly and surely inculcate good
habits. The problem is not as easy as with the

feeble-minded. The feeble-minded person of high grade when he has good habits fixed upon him becomes the victim of those good habits and will run perfectly safely until somebody leads him out of them. But the psychopath by his very constitution is not so tenacious of the habits that he has formed and may at any time break out in a new form of action. Nevertheless, it would seem that there is something to be hoped for in this direction.

To further emphasize the difference between the normally functioning mind and the abnormally functioning one and at the same time to show the readers the method of detecting abnormality we will describe the Kent-Rosanoff Association Test already alluded to. I have said that the normal functioning even of the brain is comprised within much narrower limits than is usually supposed. For example if I asked a thousand people, each to write down the first word that comes to mind when I utter a particular word, one's first thought might be that there would be a thousand different words given. Upon second thought one would see that there would be a good many cases in which two people would give the same word. But one might be quite unprepared for the statement that from seventy-five to a hundred and fifty different words would cover the entire list of

responses. Even that does not tell the whole
story. To the word "mutton" for instance, of
one thousand people, two hundred and fifty-
seven replied with the word "meat"; one hundred and twenty-one with the word "lamb";
two hundred and four with the word "sheep";
we thus have more than half of the thousand
people confined to three words, while only
thirty-six gave words that were not given by
some one else. To the word "lamp" six hundred and fifty people out of the thousand replied with the one word "light." Thus it is
seen that out of a thousand people six hundred
and fifty acted in precisely the same way in the
same situation. To revert to our word "mutton" we would all agree that "meat" or
"lamb" or "sheep" were natural and normal
reactions; also that the persons who said
"cheap," "old," or "Australia" might be perfectly normal although the words seem at first
glance a little unusual. But the person who
said "fork" or "fowl" or "mouse" or "vege-
tarian" might perhaps be thought to be a little
queer, at least we would certainly agree that
such associations are not as natural as the first
ones given. We can thus see the possibilities of
grading the normality of function of the mind.
    One word like "mutton" of course means
little or nothing but when one uses as we do in

the test, one hundred words and counts up the number of responses that have been given by a large number of people and the number that have been given by only a few people, one has, as the experiment proves, a test of the normal functioning of the mind that is of very high accuracy. For example it is found that the normal individual usually gives only from five to ten words that have not been given by somebody else while on the other hand he gives from thirty-five to forty words that have been given by more than ten per cent of the people to whom the test has been given.

As already stated this is only one of ten indications of psychopathy that we have already worked out and that are used at the Bureau of Juvenile Research.

We should not neglect the study of the physiological condition of these psychopaths. We have already spoken of several departments that were contemplated as part of the work of the Bureau, e. g., physiological or bio-chemical investigations. This involves careful analysis of the various body fluids and excreta to determine the abnormal physical conditions that underlie the abnormal conduct. If the psychopathy which makes a child act badly is due to a toxin in the blood as, e. g., the toxin of syphilis, it ought to be possible to learn something about this by careful physiological studies and thus lay the foundation for curative treatment—or else show that the condition is incurable. In other words here is a vast supply of human material upon whom experimentation is not only *justifiable*, but whose condition is such that it *demands* experimentation. It is the same situation as when a man is in severe pain and no one knows what to do. He cries out in desperation "Try something, anything to give me relief." So these children if they understood their unfortunate condition would cry out, "Try something, anything to restore us to normal boys and girls."

Now if this research work is to be done—and it is not to be forgotten that the originators of the Bureau named it a Bureau of Juvenile *Research*—then in many cases the physical rehabilitation would either be necessary or could at least go hand in hand with the research work.

It is conceivable that discoveries of profound significance to the science of medicine and to the welfare of society, would be made, in which case it goes without saying that no investment the State could make would yield such valuable returns.

# CHAPTER IV

It will be remembered that the law required that after July 1, 1914, all minors needing State care be committed to the Board of Administration. But since the Board of Administration had no place to care for them, they were sent to the Industrial Schools, the commitment reading "to the Board of Administration at its Bureau of Juvenile Research at Lancaster (Boys) or Delaware (Girls.)"

Thus only the very troublesome cases were sent to us at Columbus as we had room for them.

Section 1841-5 provides that "The Board of Administration may receive for examination *any child*, etc."

This is the *great* part of the law since it contemplates that the Bureau of Juvenile Research shall be an agency for *prevention* even more than cure. In other words we need not wait until a child has committed a misdemeanor and then examine him and find that he is feeble-minded or psychopathic and needs treatment; but we may examine him before he has gone wrong, and advise such care as will prevent him from becoming delinquent.

It is hoped that as this function of the Bureau becomes known many intelligent parents who note peculiarities in their children will avail themselves of whatever skill may be found in the Bureau personnel to explain these peculiarities. They will receive such suggestions for handling unusual children as we may be able to give. These peculiarities are not limited to bad conduct. It may be a matter of wisely guiding and educating a gifted child.

We conceive the function of the Bureau to be quite as much to help in the making of superior citizens as to prevent the development of criminals. There should be in the Bureau those who can help on the former problems quite as much as on the latter. Why should it not be so? The State Department of Agriculture works as much to help grow better corn and wheat as it does to ward off diseases that attack their plants.

A State Bureau of Juvenile Research should likewise work on the positive as well as the negative side of its problem. Many a child in the best of families has a touch of psychopathy or a physical condition, the early recognition of which may result in saving him from a break-down later, or in treatment which will result in greater efficiency and usefulness.

The precocious child and the genius are as worthy of research and study as the subnormal or the diseased.

The two clauses of the law as just explained authorize two classes of cases, which may be termed committed cases and voluntary cases. The latter group we divide for convenience into those examined at the laboratory (but not kept for continued observation) and those examined outside the laboratory—in various State institutions, County Homes, schools, and courts.

There have been three hundred and sixty-seven committed cases. These have been in residence at the Bureau cottages and under constant observation and study for periods ranging from two days to several months. The average time is about one week at present.

The voluntary cases number 3,342 of whom 1,034 have come to the laboratory for examination and 2,308 have been examined away from the laboratory. This gives as a total 3,578 cases individually examined during the two years.

It may be mentioned that besides these cases we have examined 10,800 cases by the group method. These are not considered in any of the following statistics.

The three groups should be kept carefully in mind in studying the figures, because it is obvious that they differ radically both in the sources from which they are drawn and in the completeness of the examination and the resultant value of the diagnosis.

The three hundred and sixty-seven observation cases are of course the most satisfactorily studied. The voluntary cases seen in the laboratory are as a rule more satisfactory than those examined away from the laboratory, because in the former case all the apparatus of the laboratory is available, while the test material that can be taken to a distant locality is limited.

Another item of importance that does not show in the totals but which should be kept in mind, is that throughout this two year period which has been a period of construction and organization, our method, technique and knowledge have continually improved. For example, since we have come to understand the psychopathic child, his symptoms, behavior and what we might expect from him, our time necessary for observation has diminished, our diagnoses are more accurate and our methods of handling more successful.

Some consideration also may be given to the fact that previous to January 21, 1920, we were in temporary offices and that previous to February 4, 1919, we had no observation cases because we had no accommodations for them; and that between the above dates we had only a rented house capable of accommodating only a small number of children. Even after moving into our new buildings on January 21, 1920, there was the usual "period of adjustment."

Details of the work will be found in the official report. Here are given the totals of some of the more interesting items.

The sources of the 3,578 cases are as follows:

| | |
|---|---:|
| Committed cases from Juvenile Court.......... | 236 |
| Voluntary cases referred by State Board of Charities............................... | 210 |
| Schools for Blind and Deaf.................. | 83 |
| County Children's Homes....................| 1,637 |
| Hospitals and Physicians.................... | 90 |
| Schools .................................... | 813 |
| Social Agencies ............................ | 200 |
| Miscellaneous .............................. | 75 |

Ages range from four months to nineteen years.

The misdemeanors for which the committed cases were brought into juvenile court range from "unmanageable" to murder.

The diagnoses on these cases are made in terms of intelligence level, and normality or abnormality of function. Abnormality of function constitutes psychopathy in varying degrees. A child may thus be of normal intelligence level but abnormal in function. The various combinations of these two variables will be found in report referred to above.

On account of the highly selected character of all our cases and the different bases of selection in the different groups it is not safe to draw conclusions from the percentages. But since it is of interest to see what has been found we give the percentages in each group for some of the principal diagnoses. In this table "Feeble-Minded" includes feeble-mindedness uncomplicated by psychopathy. Likewise "Normal" means of normal intelligence level and free from any psychopathy. "Psychopathic" includes every case of abnormal functioning of whatever intelligence level.

|  | Court | O. B. S. C. | State Inst. | County Homes | M. D. Hosp. | Ed. | Soc. Serv. | Misc. |
|---|---|---|---|---|---|---|---|---|
| Feeble-Minded........% | 33 | 33 | 50 | 33 | 44 | 33 | 37 | 30 |
| Deferred.............% | 17 | 29 | 7½ | 34 | 10 | 32 | 20 | 5 |
| Normal..............% | 3 | 4 | 4 | 7 | 5½ | 10 | 4½ | 13 |
| Psychopathic........% | 30 | 20 | 24 | 5 | 27 | 10½ | 20 | 23 |
| Syphilitic...........% | 8 | 8 | 7½ | 1 | 3 | 1 | 2 | 4 |

On 1,034 Lab cases the diagnoses were as follows

Feeble-Minded..........36.5

Deferred...............17.4

Normal............... 4.5

Psychopathic...........30.3

Syphilitic............. 8.

In the committed cases the Bureau must recommend to the Board of Administration a proper disposal of the case. Often the recommendation that we *would make* must be modified by what we know is possible of accomplishment. The disposition actually made of 223 Court cases is as follows:

|  | Boys | Girls | Total |
|---|---|---|---|
| Paroled to parents............... | 36 | 7 | 43 |
| Paroled to work................. |  | 2 | 2 |
| Returned to Courts.............. | 26 | 7 | 33 |
| Returned to Co. Children's Home | 3 |  | 3 |
| Assigned to I. F. M.............. | 16 | 14 | 30 |
| "      to Col. S. H. I.......... | 17 | 11 | 28 |
| "      to Cleve. S. H. I........ | 1 |  | 1 |
| "      to Massilon S. Hosp. I... | 1 |  | 1 |
| "      to Gallipolis............ | 1 |  | 1 |
| "      to State Sch. for Deaf... | 1 | 1 | 2 |
| "      or returned to O. B. S. C. | 14 | 4 | 18 |
| "      to private institution.... |  | 1 | 1 |
| "      to Boys' Industrial School | 32 |  | 32 |
| "      to Girls'    "      " |  | 26 | 26 |
| On temporary parole............ | 1 |  | 1 |
| Discharged to parent out of State |  | 1 | 1 |
| Totals.................... | 149 | 74 | 223 |

In the voluntary cases our examination is the basis for advice only. But the value of this work can hardly be over-estimated. It gives the responsible parties—parents, guardians, teachers, superintendents—valuable information as to mental ability, from which they may know the degree of responsibility, best method of treatment, dangers to be guarded against and a possible explanation of any unusual behavior. It gives the Bureau of Juvenile Research a valuable set of records for future use. Moreover some of these children will in spite of all effort get into court later and we shall then have this record with which to compare a later examination.

# CHAPTER V

The subject of the physical condition of juvenile delinquents is of the utmost importance. Perhaps not from the standpoint of its relation to the mental condition of the children themselves or to their misdemeanors; but certainly from the standpoint of its relation to the state of mind of the general public and of the parents. Physical conditions can be seen and appreciated and understood hence their amelioration is at once recognized as valuable and important work. Physical conditions are often painful, troublesome and more annoying. Their removal or cure makes the child feel happy, grateful to those who have helped him and somewhat more capable of attending to those things his caretakers would teach him. In comparatively rare instances there are physical conditions the changing of which does have marked effect upon the morals of the child. The accompanying list showing the work of our physician for two years will illustrate the foregoing statements.

No one will question the conclusion that all the physical conditions that need treatment and attention should have them; that these juvenile delinquents should be as thoroughly rehabilitated physically as medical science can do it. There has been some question as to where and when this work should be done; whether at the Bureau of Juvenile Research or in the institutions to which the child may be sent later. While it sometimes results in detaining the child at the Bureau longer than he would otherwise have to stay, yet it seems that the only sure way and the most valuable way is to have it done at the Bureau, at least until such time as it is attended to by the Court in the county from which the child is sent. One plan that has been proposed is to have two well trained and expert physicians one of whom shall diagnose the cases and provide for operations and the other shall advise and direct the work and when it becomes necessary to send patients to other institutions before the medical work has been done, this chief physician shall have the authority to follow up the cases and see that the work is actually performed. If any are to be paroled to their homes or to families, without having all their work done, the probation department will, through the help of the chief physician also see that the work is done.

Here again the greatest problem is of course the psychopath because we do not know what can be done for him; if it is a case of congenital syphilis, the anti-syphilitic treatment may be given but whether that is of any benefit has yet to be proved.

The following list shows the principal findings and indicates some of the work done at the Bureau of Juvenile Research.

460 patients examined.

177 had malnutrition.
175 had defective vision.
 28 had defective hearing.
  6 were totally deaf.
243 had carious teeth.
 72 had had dental attention.
174 had diseased tonsils.
111 had tonsils and adenoids removed.
  7 had deviated septums.
  9 had tubercular glands.
 98 had enlarged thyroids.
  2 had thyroid removal.
  9 had heart disease.
 36 had bronchitis.
  6 had active tuberculosis.
 10 were pre-tubercular.
 35 had acne.
 10 had eczema.
 16 had scabies.
 36 had pediculosis capitus.
 18 had speech defects.
  5 had operable hernia.
  1 had a brain tumor.
 67 were rachitic.

117 were round shouldered.
 29 had scoliosis.
 50 were knock-kneed.
166 were flat footed.
  3 had a tic.
 13 had epilepsy.
130 had abnormal reflexes.
 37 had positive Rosenbach.
 56 had positive Romberg.
 10 had positive Babinski.
  1 had cardiac lesion.
 20 had been circumcised.
  6 needed circumcision.
  1 had a nasal polyp.
  1 had a hemiplegia.

313 throat cultures were made.
 10 were positive.

 38 Von Pirquet tests were made.
 14 were positive.

262 urinalyses were made.
 14 were positive.

Of the 187 female patients examined:

166 had vaginal smears made.
13 were positive.

409 had blood Wassermans taken.
67 were positive.

28 surgical operations were performed.

Four hundred and sixty children had a total of 2,083 physical defects or an average of 4½ defects per child. Moreover this is a minimum because until we were well settled in our new buildings it was not possible to make the complete examination that we now make.

218 Children admitted to the Cottages have received:

301 clinical baths and 219 clinical shampoos.

106 children have been ill in the Bureau hospital a total of 347 days.

2,712 medical and surgical treatments have been given.

410 dispensary trips have been made.

1,140 treatments for syphilis—congenital and acquired.

It will be noted that the number of cases treated does not equal the number of cases needing treatment. This is because as stated above, there were no adequate facilities and no money available. We had to rely largely on the generosity of local specialists and free clinics. Often the clinics were crowded and the specialists over-run with work. There is only one way that this matter can be effectively handled and that is for the Bureau to have its own equipment and funds so that it can call in specialists as needed. A dentist could be employed and kept busy all the time. Similarly an eye, ear, nose and throat specialist.

It is probable that nothing the State could do would be so valuable as the thorough cleaning up of these physical conditions. A case from another institution well illustrates the value of this kind of work. A man was sent to the Ohio Penitentiary for non-support of his family. He had worked faithfully and supported his family until he ruptured himself. He was too poor or too ignorant to have the necessary operation. While in the penitentiary the authorities had the operation performed. The man goes out highly appreciative of what the State has done for him.

The few cases that the Bureau has been able to treat have produced a similar reaction in the parents of the children. They are grateful and appreciative and eager to co-operate. The value of this attitude cannot be too strongly emphasized.

Once let it be understood that the Bureau of Juvenile Research is a State institution created to help these families who are unfortunate in their children and the change in the attitude of this group of people toward the State institutions will be enormous. To do this the Bureau lays the emphasis on helping the child, saving him rather than on punishing him or treating him as a youthful criminal. It is to be hoped that all other institutions and agencies co-operating with the Bureau will adopt the same attitude. Why not? With the list of physical diseases and defects given above; with the mental weaknesses already described; with the environmental conditions which we all know have surrounded these children, how can we hold them responsible? How can we regard them as criminal? It is the remark of an ancient observer and quoted with approval by many thoughtful people since, that "every man is a rascal when he is sick." If sickness has such an effect upon an adult what can we expect of children?

Nor is "sickness" to be limited to conditions that result in conscious pain. No less an

authority than the late Henry Upson, M.D., of
Cleveland discovered that the painless and un-
noticed condition of impacted teeth often led to
hysteria, epileptiform outbreaks and other
nervous symptoms.  It is also recognized that
ulcerations at the roots of teeth may cause no
pain but result in forms of ''rheumatism'' and
other conditions seriously disturbing to the
normal functioning of the organism.  Dr. Henry
Cotton of New Jersey has done noteworthy
work with the insane along this line.  In the
Bureau of Juvenile Research we have already
discovered that the presence in the blood of the
poison of syphilis inherited from the ancestors
seems to lead to conduct so specific and definite
as to be of itself diagnostic—a condition almost
unbelievable.  Does not this fact alone throw a
flood of light not only upon syphilis but upon
the whole problem of delinquency?

All this but emphasizes the value of Juvenile
Courts who view their work as that of child
savers, *not* as child punishers.  They should
realize that to a large extent they deal with the
sick, not with criminals as we formerly under
stood the word.

To what extent the same holds of the adult
criminal is not for discussion here but is the
problem of the not distant future.  It may be
safely asserted that enough is already known to

warrant the State in carefully examining all its adult criminals both mentally and physically and in carefully recording the results and in modifying its treatment as the discovered facts may indicate.

This is not, as some fear, a sentimental view calculated to save criminals from the consequence of their crimes, nor an attempt to set at large, persons who are dangerous to the community. Rather is it the opposite. Not sentiment but cold reason. Not turning loose but properly guarding. It is the old method, not this new one, that keeps these dangerous persons in the community. Punishment, except for capital offenses is of limited duration. At the expiration of the sentence the individual is *free*. But he is not changed mentally or morally —unless, as is often claimed, for the worse. The new plan will not set him free until he is cured or reformed. Under the old system he leaves the institution where he has served his sentence, only to be returned to court for a new offense. Records are numerous of cases who have been at the Industrial Schools repeatedly, then at the Reformatory and finally at the Penitentiary.

I have before me a case of a boy who has been four times at the Industrial School. Examination shows he is feeble-minded. He will now go to the Institution for the Feeble-Minded where he will be cared for for life. He will be happy and useful.

Another boy has been twice to the Industrial School. He is psychopathic. As a criminal he has served his time and is free. As a psychopath he will now be sent to the State Hospital. If he can be cured of his mental disease he will go back to his home reformed, to live a life of usefulness. If he cannot be cured he remains in the institution a chronic case and the community will never again suffer from his insane pranks. If he is a real criminal—a moral imbecile perhaps—the State will never lose control of him, but will see that he is never placed where he can injure society. What more can be desired? Surely no one wants to punish these people merely for brute revenge! The only wish of everyone is to reduce crime and to protect the public.

Surely the public is better protected by keeping the mentally defective and the mentally diseased in appropriate State institutions until they are cured, if ever, than by punishing them as criminals for sixty days, twelve months or ten years and then releasing them to again prey upon society.

As a matter of fact the former method is rational. It is the latter that is sentimental albeit a hard sentiment of punishment for revenge.

Let no one think that the Bureau of Juvenile Research is actuated by any maudlin sentiment of soft sympathy or misplaced kindness. On the contrary it is an institution for the application of cold scientific rational treatment.

If it happens that rational scientific treatment proves to be less cruel than the traditional method; nay even if it proves to be a method that can effectively use methods that are kindly, that makes both officers and victims more human and less vicious, that develops whatever is good in these misdemeanants, that cares for them in a way that even makes them happy or that sends them back to society feeling that they have been justly treated and with the desire to act socially rather than anti-socially, will we complain of the method? The Javerts may drown themselves but the Abou Ben Adhems will be glad.

# CHAPTER VI

In the long run the work of such an institution as the Bureau of Juvenile Research will be judged by its results. The new method of handling cases of Juvenile delinquency may be more convenient, more expeditious or more economical but if the results should prove less satisfactory than the old way the new method must be abandoned. If the results are just as good, then the above mentioned advantages justify the change. But only if the results are far superior will the new method mark a real epoch in the development of social institutions.

In all such departments it is unsafe to draw conclusions from early results. They are often misleading. Years ago there was a theory that microcephalic idiocy was due to the too early closing of the fontanelles—the hardening of the skull before the brain had attained its full size Accordingly it was thought that an operation of cutting the skull (craniectomy) and giving the brain a chance to grow would result in an increase of intelligence. Operations were per-

formed in many institutions. For a time the results were considered highly satisfactory. But
it was found that the improvement noted was
not real but due to the fact that close watching
of the cases showed functions that though always present, had never been noticed. The
practice has long since been abandoned as a
complete failure. This is a sample of the fate
of hundreds of theories.

In a problem such as that involved in the work
of the Bureau of Juvenile Research years may
be required before we can be sure of our results
—and it may be even a generation; we may have
to wait until these children grow to adults and
try to function as normal citizens.

Nevertheless one likes to know what are the
immediate conditions following the practice of
a new method and if one does not allow himself
to draw illogical conclusions, a statement of conditions may be valuable.

It is because we feel that the public has a
right to know what we know that we record here
a brief history of some fairly typical cases.

The feeble-minded who have been fortunate
enough to be admitted at the Institution for
Feeble-Minded are settled. They are happy
and measurably useful. Society is protected
against their irresponsible offenses and against
their propagation.

Could we report that every one of the 791 cases diagnosed as feeble-minded were thus settled the State could well rejoice. Yet it is no fault of the Bureau of Juvenile Research that they are not thus provided for. But it clearly points to the need of haste in providing more institutions for this class.

One case of feeble-minded plus insanity is worth recording in some detail.

CASE I

Geo. P., age 19, was committed to the Board of Administration in August, 1919, and by them assigned to the Bureau for study.

An excellent history was obtained from a well-known social agency in the boy's native town.

On January 2, 1917, he had been arrested, charged with setting fire to a building. Being questioned he admitted this fire and *twenty-three others* causing a total loss of more than $85,000.00. He was committed by the Judge of Juvenile Court to Boys' Industrial School January 9, 1917, and released January 12, 1918. He returned to his home much to the annoyance of the citizens of that town. "All the plants on war work felt that he was a menace to the city." He was discharged from one job after another for incompetency. Finally he was arrested

July 31, 1919, for setting fire to a Doctor's office—one of several similar fires recently set in Doctors' offices. He confessed and was committed to the Board of Administration as above stated.

Upon examination he was found to be feeble-minded *and* insane. In some tests he reaches a ten-year level, in others only six. This is one of the indications of his psychopathic condition. Perhaps the ten year performance indicates the point of his mental arrest or the mentality he would have had as a feeble-minded boy if the mental disease had not set in and destroyed part of his mentality reducing him to the six year level in some functions.

Apparently the pyromania is the result of the insanity. It did not begin until August, 1917. The following is a list of his fires with estimated losses as taken from the record in the fire marshal's office:

| *Date* | | *Loss* | *Building* |
|---|---|---|---|
| Aug. 12, 1916 | $ | 10.00 | Distilled Water Ice Co. |
| Sept. 9, | ,, | 339.00 | Union Wholesale Lumber Company |
| Oct. 21, | ,, | 5.00 | Distilled Water Ice Co. |
| Oct. 22, | ,, | 2,350.00 | Union Wholesale Lumber Co. |
| Oct. 26, | ,, | 5.00 | Distilled Water Ice Co. |
| Oct. 27, | ,, | 5.00 | Parmelee Estate Building |
| Nov. 8, | ,, | 2.00 | Newark Shoe Store |
| Nov. 9, | ,, | 200.00 | John Gallagher House |
| Nov. 18, | ,, | 50.00 | L. B. Scheible |

| Nov. 1, 1916 | 75,000.00 | Albert H. Buehrle Warehouse |
| Nov. 20, '' | 100.00 | Hinely Bros. Meat Shop |
| Nov. 22, '' | 85.00 | A. Kooperman Tailor Shop |
| Nov. 23, '' | 1.00 | Lytle and Wentz Store-house |
| Nov. 23, '' | 1.00 | Hitshue Bros. Cigar Store |
| Nov. 26, '' | 100.00 | John Gallagher House |
| Nov. 26, '' | 228.00 | Car of lumber |
| Dec. 1, '' | 750.00 | Otto Schuman Furniture Store-house |
| Dec. 9, '' | 125.00 | Dalzell Bros. |
| Dec. 11, '' | 5.00 | Parmelee Estate Building |
| Dec. 21, '' | 5.00 | Parmelee Estate Building |
| Dec. 27, '' | 6,000.00 | Newark Shoe Store |
| Dec. 31, '' | 200.00 | John Gallagher House |
| Jan. 1, 1917 | 5.00 | Dalzell Bros. |
| Jan. 2, '' | 2.00 | Distilled Water Ice Co. |

These with those committed after his return from the Boys' Industrial School total $91,000.

He was committed to the Institution for the Feeble-Minded and at once transferred to the Lima State Hospital (for Criminal Insane) because his habit of setting fires made him too dangerous for the former institution.

His early history is interesting as showing how all of this loss could have been saved.

He started to school at eight years of age; was two years in first grade and three years in second grade; then passed to third "merely because he had been in second so long." "He was a harmless enough lad but never learned anything." The principal and all his teachers recognized that he was feeble-minded.

If he had been sent to the Institution for Feeble-Minded at that time he would have become a harmless inmate earning his own living under direction.

Had the Bureau of Juvenile Research not been in existence he would upon his latest arrest have been sent to the Mansfield Reformatory only to be set at liberty in due time, to repeat his criminal acts landing finally in the penitentiary for a term—"a dangerous criminal." At last he is understood and properly cared for for life. He is fairly happy and useful in the institution but not as much as though he had been sent to the Institution for Feeble-Minded when a child. Thus we learn by our mistakes.

### CASE II

Howard D., 15 years, was committed to us in February, 1919, with a continuous history of stealing, from the time he was 5 years old.

Upon examination he was found to have a mental level fully up to his age, thus neither feeble-minded nor even backward.

But the test showed a distinct psychopathic condition. After two months observation at the Bureau it was decided that the best treatment for him would be firm discipline with plenty of work and regular regimen.

He was accordingly assigned to the Boys' Industrial School.

He remained there four or five months and was allowed to go home. This was done without the knowledge of the Bureau.

A letter from his mother saying he was home was our first information. Since he was at home we decided to let him stay as long as he behaved well. His family put up with him until early in January, 1920, when they wrote us that it was impossible to handle him any longer. He was accordingly returned to the Bureau for further observation preliminary to a re-assignment.

Here he seemed to settle down and for a month or more was quite trustworthy.

Then without warning he broke. In the night he escaped from his room, entered the Administration building, stole $160.00 in cash, a lot of street car tickets, a typewriter (small Corona) and a stop watch. He went immediately home, stole all the money he could find there, got his boy scout suit and was next heard from in New Orleans from which place he sent post cards home.

This case well illustrates the limitations of the Bureau under the present plan. Had the information which the Bureau obtained been utilized and had its diagnosis been accepted this

boy would still be in the Boys' Industrial
School, carefully cared for and either improving or, if growing worse mentally, be in line to
be transferred to a more suitable institution.
Instead of that the State goes to a lot of expense
to learn his true condition and then in spite of
that knowledge turns him loose to be a greater
menace to society than he ever was before.

CASE III

Myra C., 16 years, 8 mos.  Mental age 15 yrs.
3 mos.  Talks well, adapts well to new situations
and behaves normally in many ways.

She is very hysterical, and shows her psychopathic condition by many signs.  Pretends faint-
ing spells and falls, in order to elicit sympathy.
Pretends loss of appetite but eats when unob-
served.  Makes many accusations against nearly
every one with whom she has to do.  Everybody
is supposed to be against her.

These symptoms expressing themselves in
many different forms, have existed for about
three years.

Father brought her into court in June, 1918,
because he could not control her, claims she
lies, stays out at nights, steals, forges, etc.

Has held many positions—mostly was unsat-
isfactory not so much for lack of ability as for
lack of interest.

Father and mother divorced, both diseased, maternal grandfather alcoholic.

Myra went thru the eight grades of public school, ability above average.

Was under observation at Bureau of Juvenile Research for about three months and was diagnosed as hysteria plus paranoia probably due to congenital syphilis. During the three months, she was repeatedly examined and her conduct analyzed. Finally she became interested in her own mental condition and claimed that she was tired of her old life and was going to reform.

Altho not much stock was taken in her profession it was thought best to parole her to her home. It is now two years and there has been no complaint of her conduct. It is not likely that she is "a reformed girl," but as she has grown older she may have learned to control her anti-social habits and to live within the law. It is as impossible to predict her future as it is to cure her disease. But at least enough is now known of her to serve as a guide whenever she next requires official attention, either because of misdemeanor or disease.

Later she married a young fellow who is now in State Hospital with dementia praecox. She is now working but changes jobs often.

Upton E., 19 yrs. old, is one of 15 children; two others in the Institution for the Feeble-Minded.

Upton has been incorrigible and delinquent, and has been sent to the Boys' Industrial School four times.

Finally sent to the Bureau for examination. He has the mind of a ten year old child.

His school history shows he spent five years in second grade. Says he finally got to sixth grade—if true was probably promoted on his height.

This is an interesting illustration of the trouble that can be caused by an unrecognized feeble-minded boy. He could have been recognized as feeble-minded, when in second grade of school. He is of nervous temperament, easily irritated and because of his feeble-mindedness has no control over himself. Rightly handled and treated as a ten year old boy he is tractable, well-behaved and a good worker. At the Institution for the Feeble-Minded he is contented and happy.

CASE V

Walter N., 14 years, was brought by his father. He had been a source of worry to his parents, for many years.

He was disobedient, stubborn, destructive and wilful. Though he had an excellent home, fond parents and the best of treatment from unusually intelligent foster parents, he showed no gratitude or appreciation.

Though very poor in school work, he had passed along until he was trying to do 8th grade work. Finally he threatened to do physical injury to his parents.

He was brought to the Bureau of examination. He proved to be psychopathic to a mild degree but more fundamental was a true arrest of development, giving him a mental age of about 12. He had a rather unusually good rote memory which undoubtedly explains his reaching 8th grade in school. His ability to use such facts as he had memorized was almost nil. Cannot do long division accurately or solve a simple mental arithmetic problem.

The explanation to his parents of the real condition of this boy, cleared up many difficulties.

He was placed in an environment more suitable to his condition and was happy and got along nicely.

### CASE VI

Nora S., 17 years old, has a long and pitiful history. A brief summary can only be given here.

Born in Russia, her mother died when she was three years old. Then her troubles began. Her father's housekeeper beat her, a convent abused her, an aunt in Bohemia did better. At nine her father sent for her and her brother to come to America. Their caretaker got drunk and deserted them in Prague, and Nora got lost in Bremen. She finally reached America and at 12 was trying to keep house for her father, who was drunken and far from considerate.

She was soon brought into court and adjudged "a dependent and neglected child."

The next five years were a round of placements (or misplacements) in families.

Between bad homes, Nora's undeveloped and untrained mind, her sick body and the general ignorance of her real nature, these five years form a tragic history.

Finally she was brought to the Bureau September, 1918, by the probation officer to see if we could give any advice. She "had been placed in several homes and had been found absolutely impossible in each and every one of them." She would not keep herself clean; was positively filthy; took no care of her clothing, etc., etc.

Examination by the Bureau showed her to be distinctly psychopathic. How much this condition had been aggravated by the mistreatment at the hands of the many people who had tried to care for her, but who had misunderstood her, it was impossible to say.

The first thing to do was to try to make her happy. She was found to have a strong desire to be an artist (painter). Whether this was an insane delusion—that she was artistic—we did not at first know. However, it did not take long to prove that she had real talent. She greatly improved; became clean, cheerful, interested in the future and was doing excellently at her art work, provision for which has been made so that she was devoting practically all of her time to its study.

It is evident, however, that there is a deep psychopathic condition and what the outcome will finally be no one can yet predict. At least she is at last understood, is well treated, is happy and having everything done that science can do. Her artistic talent is marked and it is greatly to be hoped that it can be saved to the world.

(Later. Nora has gone bad again and as she is now of age she is out of the jurisdiction of the State. She ran away, went to another part of the state "to save her brother from damnation." She afterwards returned and was believed to be soliciting on the street. At last accounts was employed as a telephone girl and very erratic.)

Colman, W., 13 years, 7 months. Mental age, 12.

Incorrigible. "Real causes, Mental and Physical condition." Has had St. V. dance. Breaks furniture, brandishes knife. Has been in city hospital eight times.

Committed to Bureau in May, 1919.

Mental examination showed him somewhat backward and quite psychopathic. Physical examination showed badly diseased kidneys and eight diseased teeth. The Bureau was unable to care for the teeth, since the free dental clinics are closed in summer and the Bureau has no funds for such work.

The kidney trouble was taken in hand and the child put on diet. His condition improved rapidly. At the end of six weeks he was returned to the Court and paroled to his home. Frequent letters indicate that he is getting along well.

June 14, 1918, a 16 year old girl of Slavic parentage was brought to the Bureau.

The Director being at that time the entire "personnel" of the Bureau, made the examination.

The child had been taken from her home by the court on account of attempted suicide by jumping from the third story window. Examination showed she was not feeble-minded as was feared, but was suffering from mental disturbance or psychopathy possibly induced by the beatings she had received from her father. She told a pitiful story of parental cruelty and when asked what she thought would make her happy, replied as the tears came to her eyes, "A good home." The Ohio Board of State Charities accordingly found what was thought to be a good home. But Amy's mental condition was such that she could not adjust herself to the situation. She was not truthful or honest and moreover she developed "spells," which were diagnosed as epileptic. After repeated trials in various homes she was committed to the Bureau, December 31, 1919, with the expectation that she would be assigned either to Gallipolis Epileptic Hospital or to The Girls' Industrial School.

As a result of observation in the Bureau it was suspected that the spells were hysterical in character. She was given suggestive treatment, paroled to a home where she could be under observation and further treatment by suggestion. The spells disappeared entirely and have never returned. She was somewhat longer in controlling her lying and stealing, but even that seems to have been attained. In June she was paroled, rather against our judgment, to her father who promised to treat her well.

In November, 1920, she was married and writes that she is very happy. It may be that this is a happy ending to a rather sad story. Amy certainly has not a mind of high order but if what mind she has functions normally— as it seemed to be doing when she was paroled —she may do as well as the average of her class. Children? Aye, there's the rub! But much as the idealistic eugenist would like to interfere, science has as yet no data that would warrant denying Amy these blessings.

Later: Amy's husband deserted her. She has divorced him and married another!

CASE IX

Kathryn P., 16 years. Committed for truancy and incorrigibility. Examination showed normal intelligence but psychopathic function.

However, the history of the case and behavior while under observation were encouraging. Every effort was made to make the child happy, to give her agreeable occupation and to encourage her honest efforts. In time the psychopathy cleared up and she was paroled to intelligent people who sent her to school where she did excellent work. She is now self-supporting as well as a self-respecting young woman. She is no longer a social problem.

Under the old method she would have been committed to the Girls' Industrial Home to be released in a year; perhaps, as often claimed, worse than she entered.

Tom T., 17. Committed for stealing and being in bad company. Had been at the Boys' Industrial School and paroled. Diagnosis, inferior normal in level with some psychopathy. Was paroled to work but the work was not suited to him; got into trouble again and was returned to Bureau.

Father says for past four years boy seems to have attacks about every five or six months in which he steals, is stubborn and mean. At other times he is a good worker and a good boy. There is insanity in the family.

In cottage he showed considerable mechanical skill; was untrustworthy with young children. He had a strong desire to go back home to his regular trade. He was accordingly paroled to his father. He has been home for six months and so far is doing well. He dresses nicely and keeps himself neat. If he can be kept under good influence and at work for a reasonable period will probably come out all right and be a useful citizen of moderate ability.

Scott B., 14 years. Committed for setting fires. Two physicians certified that boy was insane but the judge did not feel satisfied to send him to an insane hospital.

It is true that there is insanity in the family.

Boy had convulsions until he was five years old, said to have been of epileptic nature. Had reached sixth grade in school. Always a good boy at home and in school.

Examination at Bureau showed an intelligence level of eleven years with no sign of insanity and scarcely a trace even of psychopathy. Physical examination showed infected tonsils. These we removed. He was kept for observation four months. His behavior in the cottage was splendid all this time. We placed considerable responsibility on him. This seemed to develop in him self-respect and self-reliance.

When he spoke of the fires he said he did not know why he did it but was sure he would never do such a thing again.

We have never given any other inmate of the Bureau so much responsibility as we did this boy. He made good in it all.

Finally his father having moved to a new neighborhood we decided to parole the boy to him. It is now eight months and the reports continue to be good.

He will never be brilliant but with right treatment he will be useful. He ought never to marry unless he is sterilized but that will of course be hard to control.

We have detailed some of the results achieved by the Bureau in the case of individual children. But by far the most important achievement is a clearer view of the problem of delinquency and of the handicaps under which the State is working as a result of ignorance of the causes that lead to delinquency.

In handling the delinquent, society has followed a procedure which many of us would be the first to condemn if we saw it practiced in other lines of effort—*society has considered only the end product.*

# CHAPTER VII

Delinquency is a social disorder, a disease of the body politic. As such it should be eradicated. Can this be done?

It is now agreed that mankind is driven on, impelled to activity by reason of his peculiar structure, physical and chemical, whereby he develops energy which manifests itself in sev eral definite lines named by psychologists instincts; sometimes called the human hungers or the great human urges. These are fundamentally two—the urge or instinct of self-preservation and the instinct of race perpetuation —sex hunger.

Self preservation sub-divides into several types of action, such as *care of self* which includes all those activities which make for the comfort of the individual such as satisfying hunger and other bodily needs and providing for the future by hoarding; and *fear of enemies* which includes activities of fighting, escape, deceiving, etc.

These activities may be co-operative or antagonistic. In animals the fighting instinct is usually at the service of the sex instinct while the instinct to run away and save the self may be antagonistic to the instinct for the preservation of the race.

There is still another instinct which in man has attained large proportions and dominates all the rest. This is the hunger for companionship, the social instinct, the herd instinct among animals.

While we have herds, colonies and organized groups among animals it is the human race that has made the social organization the supreme motive. Everything yields to that. Every instinct that tends to disturb the social organization must either be eradicated or modified until it no longer endangers the group as a whole. To this end the group makes laws and punishes those who violate them.

But if the social instinct is everything, why should anyone violate the rules of the group? Why does not everyone want to do what is best for the group since in so doing he does what in the long run is best for himself?

Most people do obey the laws, but some cannot understand (these are weak minded) and others cannot control their actions (these are diseased).

What makes it specially difficult is that many of these actions that endanger the social welfare are the result of instincts as fundamental as the social instinct itself—and originally just as strong. There is no human urge more fundamental or stronger than sex. In a primitive state it was a virtue to be the parent of all the children possible. But organized society has decreed the highest welfare of the group requires that "a man shall be the husband of one wife." All else is vice—sex immorality. The instinct must be controlled.

Similarly the hoarding instinct leading to the appropriating of everything one wants, once a virtue, becomes stealing; and deceiving the enemy becomes lying.

The logical way to bring about the desired change in action is for the individual to make a bargain with himself saying: "I give up these individual indulgences in return for the benefits I derive from the social organization." But unfortunately the instincts "ripen" somewhat earlier than the reason develops whereby the youth is able to appreciate the benefits of society. Therefore the child has to be held in check by authority and fear of consequences until his intelligence develops so that he can see for himself. Meanwhile parents and teachers are doing their best to make him understand.

The *great discovery* is that there are two great groups who can never *of their own accord* conform to the rules of the group or the laws of the land—the one because they never have enough intelligence to understand the reason and the other because while they may understand, they have lost through brain disease, the power to inhibit the anti-social act.

What then will the group do about it? What it has done is organize a group of people to watch for violators of the law, arrest and punish them in the hope that the punishment will "teach them a lesson."

We now know that they cannot learn the lesson.

Why not find out who are the children who *cannot* (not *will* not) adapt themselves to the rules of the group, and take care of them before they make any serious trouble? Until recently we have not known how to detect them. But now methods are available and it is only necessary to organize the work.

It is now possible to detect by strictly scientific methods (1) those children who are feebleminded and incapable of learning; (2) those who are psychopathic and incapable of controlling their actions even when they know what is right.

This is the work for a State Bureau of

Juvenile Research, Department of Child Welfare, State Bureau of Child Husbandry, Child Conservation, Department of Paidology or whatever it may be called. Such an organization, while it would ideally be under local control —since each community should solve its own problems—should begin as a State Department under a Commissioner, Secretary or Director or else as an institution under its own Board of Directors or a Central Board of Control.

There are several objections to the last mentioned plan. A Central Board of Control having other institutions to care for, does not have the time to devote to the special problems that are constantly arising in connection with an institution that is not only new but of a wholly new type.

Secondly, it is difficult for such a Board to appropriate the funds necessary in this type of institution without arousing jealousies in the older institutions. Yet an institution for the scientific study of childhood is very different from any institution that is mainly custodial or one that deals wholly with adults. Practically every employee in a Bureau of Juvenile Research should be either a scientist or capable of appreciating the scientific attitude and of cooperating heartily with the scientific experts. In the household department from the cook to

supervisor, all should be capable of handling
and disciplining children in the most approved
manner.  Many of the misdemeanors for which
the children have been sent in are due to wrong
handling at home or elsewhere and if the specialists of the Bureau are to make wise recommendations they must know what each child is capable of under wise handling.  It is a fatal blunder
if the Bureau decides that a child is unreform-
able because the caretakers in the Bureau have
used wrong methods and aggravated instead of
improving the child's conduct while under observation.

Such intelligent caretakers cost more than the
average institution attendant, guard, nurse or
teacher.

There is one advantage of a central Board in
that it controls the institutions to which the
children are finally assigned and it can therefore insist upon complete co-operation.  This is
of vital importance if the problem of juvenile
delinquency is to be solved and an efficient system maintained.

The problems arising in a Bureau of Juvenile
Research are too intricate to be solved at a
glance.  Child nature is highly complex.  The
factors involved are numerous.  Juvenile research may involve *years* of observation.  All of
the State's machinery in all of its children's

institutions should be parts of the one system
for handling the case.

The Bureau of Juvenile Research should be
required neither to keep children in its own
wards for years nor to make final disposition of
a case before a sure diagnosis is possible. The
reasonable and economical procedure is to make
the best diagnosis possible in a reasonable time
and follow this with the best suggestion for
treatment that can be made at the time, with the
understanding that the child is still under observation and if the prescribed treatment does not
accomplish the result something else will be
tried.

For example, after observation for a week or
more the Bureau decides that the discipline,
regular life and regimen of the industrial school
may put the child into condition to be tried again
in his own home. A re-examination after a
given period should be made to discover whether
this result has been obtained. If not it is clearly
folly to send such child home.

In the Ohio plan this procedure has not yet
obtained. Children assigned to the Industrial
schools have been dismissed from these schools
without reference to the Bureau of Juvenile
Research. The result is that they are again
misdemeanants to be disposed of by the courts.
Several have been sent to the Bureau by the

courts a second time. This is only playing with the situation, it is not solving the problem. It is not using such a Bureau to the best advantage.

Another use of such a Bureau that would result in great value to the State, would be to classify the inmates of the various State institutions into normals, mental defectives and mentally diseased, thereby simplifying the problem of care, reducing the cost and helping the parole board. From the standpoint of the welfare of society this should be one of the important functions of such a Bureau. These institutions are supposed to harbor persons of normal mind and to reform them. Yet rules and methods have to be formulated to fit both the feeble-minded and the insane or psychopathic. Separated, each group would be happy and contented under rules that fitted. The normal group are as a rule trustworthy because they have intelligence enough to know what is the wisest conduct. The feeble-minded are trustworthy because it is the nature of the feeble-minded to be docile, easily satisfied and contented when well treated—treated as children. The psychopath is never to be trusted because he has no control over his impulses. Yet when it comes to parole it is the psychopath that makes the most effective appeal. His promises "ring true" because he is an actor and more because he is sincere and means what he says— *at the time.* A month later when his disease takes on an active phase he may commit any crime in the list. A fourteen year old boy at the Bureau was a model for six weeks, beloved by everybody and believed in by all who did not know he was psychopathic. Then he broke out into the vilest misdemeanors imaginable. We could have inflicted drastic punishment with a good conscience had we not realized that he was not responsible. It was the poison in his blood transmitted to him by his syphilitic mother that forced him to these unnatural acts. Is it kind either to him or to society to parole such a boy? Yet such cases are continually paroled because their true condition is not recognized.

*The Bureau in the past has assigned such cases to institutions and they have been paroled, re-arrested and re-committed to us within four months.*

Some states are proposing to place such a Bureau under the control of the State University. This has the advantage that the scientific needs will be appreciated and broad policies established. If the needed co-operation in assigning the children, can be established this would seem to be a satisfactory procedure.

Another plan has been proposed, viz: that of having the Bureau and all children's institutions under one Board of control, who would thus be able to concentrate on the one group of problems pertaining to the state's children. This plan might work best of all especially if such Board were composed of men and women of broad views and devoted to child welfare.

Under the reorganization law which went into effect July 1, 1921, Ohio is in a position to work out the problem of its delinquent, dependent, and defective children with a high degree of efficiency. The Ohio Board of Administration with four members has been replaced by the Department of Public Welfare with a single responsible head—the Director. This Department also takes over the work of the Board of State Charities and the Parole Board.

Thus the Director of Public Welfare controls all the States' wards, the institutions and agencies dealing with them. He can thus bring about the highest co-operation in accordance with a broad plan. He can command the services of the Bureau of Juvenile Research for all wards and use the results of its examinations not only to improve the condition of each state ward but to better protect the state from the irresponsibles.

His chief of the Medical Staff can unify the medical work on all cases.

His Chief of Parole and Probation can exercise real care and oversight over all state wards that have been allowed to leave the various institutions. This has never been possible under the old system. It may be questioned whether any institution can adequately handle its cases after they are paroled or placed on probation. There are too many conflicting interests and it is too likely to become a side issue to the main work of the Institution.

When a child or adult is committed to the care of the state, the state takes the place of the parents and should exercise all the care and interest of a wise and fond parent. It is not a matter of punishing and turning loose. It is a matter of bringing up the child until the child needs no further care. If that time never comes, it means life care.

The *method* and *kind* of care is for the state to determine just as the parent determines for his child. In a good family the child is kept in the home until his ability and favorable circumstances warrant his going out for himself, at first under the oversight and control of the parents and later entirely on his own responsibility. The proper time for this independence, the intelligent parent discovers by careful *study* of his child.

Likewise the state should keep its children in its various "homes" as long as necessary, then put them out on probation until they demonstrate their ability to take their places as full fledged free citizens. The attitude should always be *fond care for the welfare of the child* (adult in years though he be) and *never* the attitude of desiring to get rid of the child at the expense of the welfare of the community and the child.

We have had too much of the idea that these state wards are a burden and an expense. In one sense they are. So is every child. But what true parent ever thinks of his children in those terms? Why should the State? These children are here in our midst and we put our heads in the sand when we think that we escape the burden and the expense when we turn them loose upon society *before* they are able to function as normal citizens.

Not only must we take adequate care of all who now become legal wards of the state, but the time must soon come when we will take many children from their parents and make state wards of them because the parents are found to be incompetent and are bringing their children up to be anti-social beings.

It is better and in the end cheaper for the State to do this than to wait until these children become vicious and anti-social adults.

This does not say that the public should support as a State ward every child whose parents would merely shirk their responsibility as parents. That is already an evil.

John J. of ———— has three children, his wife is dead. He has married again but his second wife does not want the children so he has placed them in a County Home at public expense. This should not be tolerated and need not be. But legitimate State wards must be adequately cared for. This can be done by such an organization as Ohio now has.

We have raised the question earlier of the physical rehabilitation of the children committed to the Bureau of Juvenile Research. The broad view of the Bureau set forth in this chapter makes an easy and satisfactory solution of that problem.

The Bureau should be responsible for such work. It should be amply equipped to do everything that needs to be done. But whenever it is more feasible to have the work done elsewhere the Bureau should have authority to make the necessary arrangements. The one thing of paramount importance is that someone is responsible for having these physical handicaps attended to.

The other matter referred to above, is the care of the psychopathic child. According to such figures as we have the number of these cases is large. There are indications that they divide into three groups: First those who deteriorate rather rapidly either (a) to a low level of mentality or (b) to a definite insanity. The former are now cared for with the feeble-minded and may so continue without serious inconvenience. The latter can go of course to the hospital for the insane. Second, is the group that stands still; and third, are those that seem to outgrow the condition.

An institution for psychopathic children is the rational solution. These cases need to be studied and curative treatment discovered if possible. Many of them seem to be due to congenital syphilis. Anti-syphilitic treatment should be given. Valuable discoveries for the handling and treatment of these cases may reasonably be expected.

Until such an institution can be established the industrial schools and reformatories could do much by having departments for such cases and employing specialists to do such work for them as may prove possible. Here again the larger function of the Bureau of Juvenile Research would insure the most efficient handling of this problem.

Whatever be the name of this state agency, its function as a research body should never be lost sight of. While our knowledge of the problem has greatly increased in the past few years there are still scores of lines along which we need information.

One of the most promising fields of medical research today is the so-called glandular therapy. There are many indications of glandular disturbances in delinquents. A physiological laboratory with a trained bio-chemist in charge is on our program. This is only one of many lines of research that may be expected to yield valuable information that will help us to restore these delinquents to useful citizenship.

We have also alluded to the fact that an ideal handling of the problem of delinquency would be by the local authorities. Though this is not feasible at once, it should be the function of a state Bureau to encourage, develop and foster this procedure.

The Ohio Bureau of Juvenile Research is already moving in that direction. The first thought about the Bureau was that all juvenile court cases committed to the Bureau should be sent to Columbus. This is expensive and has some other disadvantages. To obviate these we have established sub-stations or clinics in three cities where we send examiners one or two days a month, and have arranged to co-operate with local examiners in other cities. It may well be

that in time these cities—and others—will take
over this work and manage their own problems.
It may still be "The Ohio Bureau of Juvenile
Research" by the simple expedient of our recognizing the examiners as nominally members of
our staff—if that is necessary or desirable.

Another phase of the work of such a Bureau
should be the examination of *all* children who
come before the juvenile court. This could come
under the voluntary clause since undoubtedly
any judge would welcome such help. The point
is that first offenders are not usually sent to a
state institution hence are not committed to the
Bureau of Juvenile Research, yet the feeble-
minded child and the psychopath are just as
defective on their first offense as later and
should of course be recognized as needing care
and be provided for without waiting until they
prove their abnormal condition by repeated
offenses. Moreover this would give us the case
at an earlier age when there is a better prospect
of effecting a cure or reform by establishing
good habits before the bad ones become too
strong.

The next step should be to arrange for the
mental examination of every possible suspect.
This would take the matter back to the public
school. A psycho-clinician and a physician in
every school system with authority given to the

Superintendent or Board of Education to carry out the recommendations of such clinician and physician would be a logical procedure which would attack the problem at the roots. When once established on an efficient basis juvenile delinquency would nearly all disappear.

# CHAPTER VIII

No study of delinquency will every adequately
cover the ground that does not give a large
place to congenital syphilis. And no system of
handling delinquents will ever be successful that
does not first discover all those who are suffering from congenital syphilis and treat them in
accordance with the lessons that have been
learned as to the influence that that disease has
upon conduct and character. It would perhaps
be hard to find a subject of such importance that
has been so thoroughly neglected as congenital
syphilis. Perhaps this is not surprising when
we recall that even active, or acquired syphilis
as it is called, has been until recently kept so
secret that no one had an accurate idea of its
prevalence or much notion of its effect. Often
treated by quacks and patent medicines the
reputable physician saw relatively few cases
and when he did, he was bound by the bond of
secrecy and kept in every way from investigat-
ing the antecedents and consequences in any

particular case. That is now being changed and
we are discovering some of the things that lie in
the wake of this greatest scourge of the human
race.

Not the least of the multitude of serious consequences of this disease is the fact that it leaves
its victim more or less incapable of transmitting
a healthy constitution to its offspring. Here
again we can speak only in the most broad and
general terms. For it is a comparatively short
time that scientists have been studying this
problem and consequently have no accurate
figures. Guesses range all the way from the
most appalling percentages, to comparatively
insignificant ones. For example it has been said
that no individual who has had active syphilis is
ever so completely cured that he will not trans-
mit the evil effects to any offspring that he may
have. While at the other extreme are those who
have come to the conclusion that it does not
amount to much anyway. As usual the truth
probably lies somewhere in the middle ground
though it is somewhat discouraging to find that
the more studies that are made the more serious
is found to be the situation. Apparently there
are many degrees and conditions of infection
and we are in great need of numerous careful
studies on the various phases of the problem.
We cannot go into that at this time and can only

point out that congenital syphilis is very prevalent among juvenile delinquents and that it has very typical effects upon conduct as well as upon mental function.

We have sufficient evidence to make it entirely probable that the poison of this disease affects the growth of the embyro in such ways that the groups of more delicate nerve cells are more or less seriously affected; with the result that normal functioning is disturbed. Nor has the range of conduct that is attributable to this disease as yet been studied. But enough is already known to make it reasonably safe to conclude that *when there is syphilis in the parents* and *persistent bad conduct in the child* we are dealing with cause and effect and all treatment and handling of the child must take into account this condition.

It must not be forgotten that the methods of determining congenital syphilis are very inadequate at present and it may well be present in many cases where none of the usual evidences are found. For example it is now generally agreed that the absence of a positive Wasserman blood test is very slight evidence that the individual is free from the disease. Southard is on record as declaring that a negative Wasserman means nothing; but that a positive Wasserman means about ninety percent accuracy.

Hardly anybody claims that a negative is more than fifty percent accurate. Moreover it is now well known that the old pathonomonic signs may be entirely wanting and yet the child show in his behavior and in his psychological test every indication of suffering from the effects of this disease, which in many cases has been proved to have been present in the parents.

Healy wrote* six years ago as follows: "It is clear that when the central nervous system is much affected or when there is a sensory defect as the result of congenital syphilis, the relationship of the disease to delinquency may be close." But we now know that the relationship is close when there is no sensory defect and when the central nervous system cannot be seen to be much affected.

In the judgment of the writer we have only begun to scratch the surface of this problem of congenital syphilis and its effects; and further study will show that a surprisingly large proportion of delinquency is due to this disease. Why may it not be so? If one believes firmly in the uniformity of nature that the same cause produces the same result one cannot escape the conclusion that a normal brain, functioning normally produces normal conduct and that where abnormal conduct is found there must be some disturbing factor that interferes with normal

*Individual Delinquent, page 205.

function. And where the abnormal conduct is as uniform as it is in many cases of delinquency, it is entirely reasonable to think that there may be one and only one cause for the disturbance. We do not wish to be understood as arguing that all delinquency is due to congenital syphilis; but only that there are certain types of conduct and certain peculiarities of function, as determined by psychological tests, that may be very easily attributed to this one cause. This much seems highly probable. The effect of this discovery, if it proves to be such, upon our treatment and understanding of delinquency must be far reaching. It will signalize the passing of the day when we are limited to the study of individual symptoms with the attempt to reform each child by a special application to his individual needs or what seems to be his symptoms; and the entering into a phase of the situation where we say: "It is not the problem of finding some way of disposing of this individual delinquent so that his peculiarities will be provided for, but it is a case of recognizing that he is a congenital syphilitic and as such none of the usual methods is more than palliative. We only attain to the results that we seek with this type when we have learned how to control congenital syphilis.

Finally, we have already said that there is no idea of maintaining that all delinquency is due to congenital syphilis. But just as it seems likely to be proved that one type of delinquency is due to this disease, so we should look for the causes of other types which in turn must be understood and controlled. In other words not *symptoms* but *etiology* seems to be the line of approach to this problem as it has been most successfully done in many other forms of disease. This has been the history of medicine and sociology may well learn the lesson and profit from this experience of the older science.

# CHAPTER IX

The question inevitably arises, how snall the
problem of delinquency be handled by the state
or by local community? This is a part of the
much larger question, that of centralized
government. The Ohio Bureau of Juvenile Research is a State institution but the question is
sometimes asked, why should not each county
or each municipality have its own Bureau? The
question is more frequently asked in connection
with the matter of expense of sending children
from the far distant counties to the capital of
the State for examination. The same question
might as well or even better be asked in regard
to the institutions for the feeble-minded. Why
should they be State and not county institutions? We do not propose to discuss the question extensively here but only to state that there
are many arguments in favor of local communities handling all of these problems.

Of course the objection is the usual one that

many local communities would neglect the problem and then their neighbors would suffer. A part of these at least could be obviated by having central inspection much as we have in the public school system. It is often asked why we have state institutions for the feeble-minded. The answer sounds rather amusing not to say ridiculous. State institutions were established at the time when it was thought that a small institution conveniently located would easily take care of all the mental defectives in the state. The idea that any county or group of two or three counties had enough of these inadequates to make it worth while to have a local institution was absurd. We see how increased knowledge of the situation changes the whole subject.

It may be difficult to change over from a plan of State institutions for defectives and for the insane to county or community institutions but in the matter of delinquency the machinery for local control is very largely in existence at the present moment. That machinery is the public schools. We have already defined delinquency as failure to keep up with the requirements of the group; delinquency is thus a social fault, not an individual one. Man, as explained above, is impelled to action by great internal driving forces called the great human urges or the great human hungers or by the psychologists the human instincts. We have developed these instincts because they were useful at one time; but as we follow the development of the instincts we discover the curious fact that one of these instincts has outstripped all the rest. Today the social instinct is by far the strongest force impelling civilized man. Impelled by this instinct men have chosen to live together in groups. We have practically agreed to act in groups and even think in groups. So that today for a man to take a stand for action or thought against that of the group is sometimes accounted for bravery and nobility and sometimes for insanity. So "grouped" have we become in our activities and in our thought of the material world that even individuality and initiative are almost extinct. Individuality has a hard struggle because of the strong instinct to do and say and think what the crowd thinks and says and does. In all of our acquired activities and thoughts it is easy to conform to the group. Indeed as already stated it is easier than it is to stand out by one's self. When the demands of the group run counter to the old primitive instincts we are bound to have a struggle. Now the strange fact is that the very existence of the group requires action that is counter to the primitive instincts in many instances. For example lying, stealing, sex activity are all primitive instincts and as such are powerful forces in every individual. But it does not require the highest intelligence to discover that we cannot have a social organization and practice these other instincts. The group can only exist when it works harmoniously; there can be no harmonious co-operation when we deceive each other; there can be no co-operation as long as we steal from each other. Likewise the group has determined that the gratification of the sex instinct must be controlled according to a certain rule.

It is these outbursts of the old instincts which are supposed to be controlled, that lead to delinquency. The juvenile courts are dealing with stealing, sex violations and other activities where the self has gone counter to the group. To make this adjustment between the other instincts and the social instincts requires as a rule more intelligence than is possessed by the human youth. Hence if we are to avoid trouble and provide for the welfare of the group, we must as in all such cases proceed to train the youth and induce him by means of arguments which he can understand to do these things which he does not understand but which he will appreciate later. For this purpose we have schools.

In other words the first business of the schools is to socialize the child. By socializing we must not mean the crowding together in ever larger and larger groups nor the process of making man more "sociable." The socialization of the child consists in so transforming him that his individual impulses are largely supplanted; or replaced by desires and actions that fit in with the work of the group. So modify primitive instincts that the group can function as a unit; harmoniously, exactly, efficiently and reliably—that is with no exception, like the organs of the body. It is not sufficient that each organ be healthy but each one must function in such a way as to fit in with the functioning of the rest to the end that the total functioning of the body may be that of the highest efficiency.

The socialization of the child in this sense is not only the greatest problem but of such relatively greater importance that one might say it is the only problem of the schools. If the school does not teach a child to be honest and to be moral in a strict sense of that term, that is, to live in accordance with the customs, the rules, the conventions that society has laid down, then the group which supports such a school is not only wasting its money and effort but it is committing suicide. The children who come out of such schools are individuals whose every activity will be consciously or unconsciously aimed at the welfare of society.

The school must socialize its pupils but to do this the item of first importance is to know its material.

We have been discussing the feeble-minded and the psychopath as they are found among delinquents. It should not be forgotten that these same delinquents were once found in our schools. The twenty-two hundred men in the Ohio Penitentiary were once children in school; the two thousand men in the reformatory were once children in the schools of Ohio; the twelve hundred boys and six hundred girls in the Industrial Schools were once pupils in the schools of Ohio. Or if you prefer to look into the future we can say without fear of contradiction that the children in the schools of your state, today, will some of them one day be in the penitentiary or in the reformatories or in the industrial schools—or in all of them. There are four hundred men in the Ohio penitentiary today that have been at the industrial schools or at the reformatory or both.

Clearly the schools in the past or in the present have not and are not socializing their pupils in the sense in which we have used that term. Why not? One reason is that they have not known and do not today understand fully the nature of the children in their care. We have until very recently lived and worked under the assumption that all children have the capacity to become scholars or to attain to the highest position in the land. We are fast growing out of that; we are recognizing the feeble-minded and we are clamoring for institutions in which to take care of them. As yet, however, we know almost nothing of the more dangerous type which we have described as the psychopath. The Government has shown us as the result of its testing of one million, seven hundred thousand soldiers, that ten percent of the population has a capacity for developing only a mentality of ten years or less; that another fifteen percent has approximately eleven years capacity; that there are twenty percent more of twelve years; while twenty-five percent is the great middle average with the intelligence of thirteen or fourteen year old children. Above the average we have sixteen and a half percent with a mentality of fifteen year old children; and nine percent with a mentality of sixteen and seventeen; and four and a half percent with a mentality of eighteen or nineteen years which is the highest. Now those figures apply to our schools as well as to the population of the country or to the army. And any teacher may look over his group and divide them up according to those figures. Of course less and less strictly as the numbers are reduced. But the problem of the schools today is not only to socialize its pupils, your children and mine, but it is to socialize the pupils who have only ten year intelligence and the other groups who have eleven, twelve and so on.

In the present stage of our knowledge of the evolution of the human mind it seems fairly certain that it requires at least twelve year intelligence to be able to understand abstract principles; that consequently we shall never succeed in socializing those people whose capacity is less than twelve years by any of the methods now in vogue in our schools. It can only be done by training them in definite concrete work with their hands and teaching them such elements of truth and honesty as they themselves can experience. The story of the accomplishment of children in every school in the country confirms this statement. Thirteen percent of them do not get above the fourth grade, another thirteen percent do not get above the fifth grade, fourteen percent do not get above the sixth grade and twenty-seven percent more do not get beyond the eighth. The reason being that each group has reached the limit of its intelligence. Is it not obvious why we have so many juvenile delinquents? Indeed is it not amazing that we do not have more when we think that twenty-five percent of the school children do not have a mentality above eleven years; that in spite of the fact we have been holding them in school, trying to teach them the higher branches; that we send them out of school not able to earn a living through anything that they have learned in school; that we have not succeeded in socializing them at all in the sense in which we have defined that term: that consequently they go out with the old primitive instinct of lying and stealing, sex aberrations entirely uncontrolled? This in the case of the feeble-minded.

In the case of the psychopaths we have taught them the geography and the arithmetic and the history that we set out to, but we have not socialized them because we have not understood their condition and our time has been occupied in correcting their misdemeanors in school. They have been punished again and again until they feel disgraced and unjustly treated, they leave school feeling that they are against the government. Such in brief would seem to be the situation. It is nobody's fault but our own and perhaps not ours. We have all done the best we knew but certainly we have come now to a point where we know enough about it to realize that the one thing to be done next, is to study the problem, to understand the children as well as we can and do the best possible for them. While teachers and school men are not responsible for the failure of the school in the past they will be responsible in the future if they do not devote some of their energy to educating the public to understand this problem and to provide the machinery necessary to prevent delinquency rather than waiting and establishing machinery such as juvenile courts and Bureaus of Juvenile Research to cure delinquency.

# CHAPTER X

CONCLUSION AND RÉSUMÉ

The problem of juvenile delinquency is solvable. There is no longer any need for hit or miss guesswork procedure. Scientific handling is entirely within reach.

The first step is a change of attitude whereby we regard the delinquent not as a child to be punished but as one to be treated and trained.

To this end everything that savors of punishment or carries a stigma should be abolished. State institutions might well be called State schools—the name of the city being sufficient identification. Even the word "committed" might be replaced by "assigned" or "admitted." The few cases that are found to be responsible and deserving of punishment would still be committed to a penal institution.

Children "admitted" to these schools should remain until they graduate, i e., until they are ready to take their places in society. In the case of the imbecile and the seriously psychopathic this time may never come.

Another group may have to return to the school through failure to make good.

The Bureau of Juvenile Research is the State examining board, its recommendations carrying weight in proportion as results show its trustworthiness. It is also a department of reference for help and advice to any citizen who has the responsibility of bringing up a child.

These children belong to the State because their parents have proved unwilling or unable to train them into good citizens. The State cannot afford to neglect to protect itself by adequately caring for them.

Assigning these children to an institution for a year or for any definite period is as sensible as assigning an insane man to a State Hospital for a year. He is committed until in the judgment of competent authority he is fit to return to society. That may be in a month, in a year or never.

Juvenile delinquency can be largely eradicated.

THE END

*Reprinted in Saxony by the "Obral" process for*
KEGAN PAUL, TRENCH, TRUBNER & CO., LTD., LONDON